MiS 86/32

Applications of Psychology for the Teacher

DENNIS CHILD

Professor of Educational Psychology,
University of Leeds

HOLT, RINEHART AND WINSTON
London · New York · Sydney · Toronto

Holt, Rinehart and Winston Ltd: 1 St Anne's Road,
Eastbourne, East Sussex BN21 3UN

British Library Cataloguing in Publication Data
Child, Dennis
  Applications of psychology for the teacher.
  1. Educational psychology
  I. Title
  370.15   LB1051
ISBN 0–03–910675–6

Typeset by Georgia Origination, Liverpool.
Printed in Great Britain by Biddles of Guildford Ltd.

Last digit is print no: 9 8 7 6 5 4 3 2 1

Contents

Preface

Trying to bridge the gaps between theories, research findings, the wealth of experience within the teaching profession and the practicalities of organising learning and teaching experiences for student-teachers has been a tantalising problem for those responsible for training teachers. There is so much to be done in the short period of professional training, particularly for those taking PGCE courses, that there is no time for excesses of theory *or* of undirected practical experience. Every experience has to count and be exploited.

Having written a basic textbook, *Psychology and the Teacher*, I am especially conscious of the serious difficulties facing student-teachers and their tutors in trying to assimilate so much in so little time. In fact, the book was written with more than student-teachers in mind; its aim is also 'to introduce teachers to elementary ideas in psychology which have some relevance to their work with young people'. Therefore the student teacher has to be selective in order to make the best use of the text.

The central purpose of this adjunct to *Psychology and the Teacher* is to link particular parts of the theory and the Enquiry and Discussion sections with activities which students might engage in during their various kinds of contact with learners. It is also intended to help students understand the variables that underlie successful teacher–child interaction and thus to develop strategies of their own design to fit specific teaching situations. In effect, it is a manual of suggestions for students which they can use to explore and expand on the issues raised in *Psychology and the Teacher*. It is *not* a school practice guidebook, although it would be impossible not to overlap with some ideas expressed in current published guidebooks.

School block practice is the time-honoured way of enabling students to sample *some* of the important problems of learning and teaching. I use the word 'some' because the experiences which students meet on a block practice are peculiar to the circumstances in which they find themselves. The area, the *modus operandi* of the school (streaming, open plan, etc.), the subjects taught, the ages and classes taken, the disciplinary ethos, and so on are all variable. On any one practice it is unlikely that a student will meet more than a small sample of possible experiences. In addition, the relentless grind of taking classes on a regular basis on school practice does limit the amount of reflective experimentation that can take place. But there are alternative ways of gaining practical opportunities, and this book will also direct attention to these.

Deciding on an order of presentation is always a difficult task for an author, particularly in a subject as complex as psychology. I have tried in this book to unfold the issues in a logical order, but at the same time I realise that most of the topics interrelate. Cross-referencing has been used to overcome this problem. The first chapter introduces the student to questions about the role of a student-teacher, the practical experiences offered and how they might be utilised, some of the expectations of training institutions, and how the student can capitalise on psychological knowledge to help his or her understanding of teaching and learning.

The remaining chapters follow a logical sequence. Chapter 2 deals with the kinds of considerations necessary before one ever enters a classroom. It looks at those characteristics of learners about which it is useful to know something before or during the early stages of teaching. Chapter 3 gives some pointers to teaching-practice schemes of work and lesson plans. It concentrates on aspects of preparation and planning. Chapters 4 to 6 enter the classroom and in turn consider the organisation of learning, class management and relationships, and finally, assessment and evaluation of learning and teaching. There are numerous cross-references to the basic textbook, *Psychology and the Teacher*, which is abbreviated to *PAT*.

Each chapter is punctuated with suggestions of activities for the student under such headings as practice and observation, discussion and analysis, and references. The reading is kept to a minimum, as the cross-referencing to *PAT* will give ample reading material, should students wish to expand their knowledge further.

Writing a book about an intensely human activity such as teaching cannot be a solo affair. I am truly grateful to all those colleagues, students and pupils without whose critical advice I could not have shaped this work. I am also very thankful that my daughter, Louise, relieved me of the arduous task of typing the script.

University of Leeds   *Dennis Child*
September 1985

1

Applying Psychology in the Classroom

INTRODUCTION

The commonest complaint one hears from students in teacher-training is that there is too much theory to be taken on board in the short time available for training. In addition, they feel that some of the theory seems obscure and removed from the realities they meet during school practice. To some extent, this is fair comment. It has to be acknowledged that some theories have not been cast in a form which makes them readily applicable. Others do not have direct practical aspects of relevance in education. Such theories are background information for those who wish to pursue the discipline in greater detail. But for the beginning teacher there must be careful selection of a manageable portion of relevant theory, sufficient to enable the new teacher to make reasoned decisions at the outset of teaching. The choice of what counts as relevant theory is a matter of judgement by the tutor. It is hoped that this book will act as a guide in that choice.

Having decided what can be of value, the next step is to consider how best it can be presented and put to the test. However, we can assume that students have already formulated theories of their own. Indeed, we have all generated theories about, for example, learning, memory, and intelligence, having experienced years of formal education. Our lives consist very largely of formulating and acting on generalisations built up from personal and shared experience. Student-teachers have already been in the educational system for at least twelve years and many have formed firm ideas about psychological issues. These ideas, even if not beneficial, will be hard to change unless convincing evidence, largely through practical experience, is presented and tried out to the satisfaction of the student.

Thus we bring to any practical session a number of well-established beliefs as well as, one would hope, an open-mindedness about new ideas. In the end, the most effective way of arriving at conclusions that will help in our teaching must be discovered by hammering out the problem on the anvil of experience under guidance. This is more easily said than done. It is not possible to present a student with every conceivable educational situation. We must settle for a selection of starters. Unfortunately, the conventional block school practice is rarely the best way of offering guided practice. Most feel thrown in at the deep end. The block practice should really be the climax of a systematic training programme and not the only source of experience and opportunity for trying out alternative ideas. School practice is in some cases restricting as a learning device, because the hurly-burly of classroom life or the pressure to cover the syllabus with a wide ability range do not leave much time for reflection and experimentation. Other learning experiences must be devised and this book will also stress some of these alternatives.

HOW TO USE THIS BOOK

The content has been pruned back to the bare essentials. I am conscious of the fact that students have limited time in which to absorb the wide range of material presented to them. Better to cover the most important parts of psychology and leave the rest for some later opportunity than to smother the student with too much information – to the point of suffocation. Careful selection and negotiation between student and tutor are going to be essential.

References

Where more background and theoretical knowledge is needed there is a cross-referencing system to *Psychology and the Teacher* (R1), which is abbreviated in this text to *PAT*. In the body of the text, the clue to either a cross-reference or reference to another textbook is the symbol R, followed by the number of the reference. These references are collected together at the end of each chapter. Thus, if you look for R1 under References at the end of this chapter (p. 18), you will find the full details of *PAT*.

Practice and observation, discussion and analysis

Chapters are broken down into sections, which cover major topics. In these sections are recommendations for *practice and observation activities*, signified by P, and *discussion and analysis activities*, signified by D, both followed by page numbers referring to this volume. Ps and Ds are numbered in the same way as references and they can be found on the pages indicated, in boxes. There are many suggestions. In certain circumstances some may not be possible, but some adaptations could be worked out by the tutors and students.

APPLICATIONS OF PSYCHOLOGY TO LEARNING AND TEACHING

In Chapter 1 of *Psychology and the Teacher* (*PAT*, R1) the concerns of psychology and its contribution to education are discussed. There we saw that in applying educational psychology, we hoped it would give us a means of appraising individual children's similarities and differences, and thus enable us to create more efficient learning environments for them. It provides us with a means of making evaluations of our own strengths and weaknesses as learners and teachers. Many theoretical models are presented in *PAT*, some as background information, others of immediate use.

At the heart of our needs from psychology is an abiding interest in the quality and quantity of learning by our pupils. This would be mainly academic learning, although some portion of formal education is also devoted to physical, social, emotional and moral learning. Nevertheless, the central *activity* of the formal educational system as we know it is intellectual learning. Furthermore, although the purposes behind a state system will vary from place to place and time to time, many of the fundamental problems with which teachers have to grapple will remain much the same.

Perversely, this book starts where *PAT* ended – in a consideration of curriculum matters. This is not so surprising. If we are talking about the practice of teaching, we are never far away from such questions as what should we teach, how will we teach it and what should we know about the learners. Those familiar with curriculum-planning schemes will have no difficulty in appreciating how important it is to have any learning/teaching experience well organised. In Chapter 16 of *PAT* on the curriculum process, we outlined four elements in the construction of a curriculum suggested by Tyler (R2). These were:

(a)   What educational purposes should the school seek to attain?
(b)   What educational experiences can be provided that are likely to attain these purposes?
(c)   How can these educational experiences be effectively organised?
(d)   How can we determine whether these purposes are being attained?

Translated into classroom terms and focusing on those aspects where psychology can help, the above suggestions can be reshaped into important questions which involve the teacher in decision-making:

(a)   What do I want the children to learn?
(b)   What will they need to know and do in order to learn it?
(c)   What will I need to know and do in order to help them learn it?
(d)   How will I know they have learnt it?
(e)   What must I do in the future to make my teaching of the topic more effective?

The teacher-training programme should, amongst other things, ensure that all students on qualifying are able to make reasoned decisions about these five questions. A document (R3) from the Council for National Academic Awards (CNAA – the body which, amongst other things, validates public-sector qualifications leading to a teacher's certificate), entitled *Perspectives on Postgraduate Initial Training*, proposes that a PGCE should be 'preparing beginning teachers to teach something of value that can be learnt by pupils in primary and secondary schools as they exist today; organising and managing those classrooms and controlling pupils in them; and also providing school experience programmes that underpin this'.

For ease of handling and presenting the extremely complex issues involved in the questions above, we will cast it in a form which highlights those aspects affecting *learning by the pupil* and *teaching by the teacher* (the terms 'learning' and 'teaching' being used in the broadest sense).

Learning
Consideration given to:
(a)   What are the factors we need to know before learning begins?
(b)   What would be the best organisation of the learning environment?
(c)   What outcomes are there for the learner and how are they assessed?

Teaching
Activities for:
(a)   Preparing and planning (preactive instructional management)

(b)   Creating and managing the learning environment (interactive instructional management)
(c)   Evaluating the teacher's part in learning and teaching effectiveness

These two sets of issues overlap and we shall try to account for this in the subsequent pages of the book. They constitute the major concerns of the book. Chapter 2 will look at what sorts of things we should try to discover before a lesson or other learning experience begins (learning (a)). Chapter 3 deals with preparation and planning (teaching (a)). Chapter 4 considers the criteria useful in the organisation of conditions for learning by our pupils (learning (b)). Chapter 5 is intended to take a closer look at the role of the teacher as a manager of learning, particularly the relationships in class (teaching (b)), and Chapter 6 deals with assessment in both the learning and the teaching (learning (c) and teaching (c)).

THE TRAINING PROCESS

Let us apply the above criteria to the process of training teachers. After all, it is a 'learning environment' with its own curriculum processes and the above outline should have some relevance to training. Students are learners and the tutors are teachers. Therefore the six issues above should, to some extent, be applicable to teacher-training. We shall look particularly at '*learning* (a), (b) and (c)', as outlined above, as they apply to students in training.

What does the student bring to training?

When we come to examine the factors which students might investigate about their pupils, such details as previous knowledge and experience will enter into consideration. What you bring to professional work is equally important. The subjects studied in the past for 'O', 'A' and, perhaps, degree level, the school and university experiences as a student, home influences such as study methods or parental discipline, previous teachers who might have acted as models which you may consciously or inadvertently copy, communication skills, your views about educational issues – learning, 'the system', etc. – will all predispose you towards a style of teaching. Studies of these and other student 'entry characteristics' are long overdue. There seems to be an implicit assumption that a student-teacher begins training with a 'clean slate', but experience in dealing with students soon reveals some fixed ideas and strategies for coping with problems. Those habits of decision-making which are not helpful in teaching are sometimes very difficult to alter and methods have to be developed to reverse them. Other completely new techniques need to be thoroughly established by carefully planned episodes of teaching experience.

Decision-making in the cut-and-thrust of the classroom has often to be spontaneous. Your existing predispositions, attitudes and habits often spring into the action you adopt. The functions of the college course will be to provide you with opportunities to examine your methods and the underlying assumptions, and to *inform* your decisions (D1, p. 9).

Learning environments for students

In order to expose faulty decision-making or afford opportunities for rehearsal of good practices, what 'environments' can be created for the student? Lectures, tutorials and seminars will help to give theoretical and research background, but actual guided experience is the only way of establishing good practice. Inevitably, courses have a teaching-practice system, usually a block practice plus a range of other practical experiences. As mentioned earlier, the block practice is really an approximation to the real thing and offers few chances for the student to try out, experiment (and make mistakes!) and rehearse particular aspects of teaching with enough time to reflect on the results. The possibility of isolating teaching difficulties or trying out a teaching skill should be available in forms of teaching experience other than the block school practice.

The ideas expressed in this book are purposely designed to extend beyond the conventional practice. They would have to be tried out during the many other opportunities when students can 'practise' in various kinds of learning environments. This is the only way in which theoretical propositions can be verified. Both theory and practice are vital. Misguidedly, some institutions think they have found the solution to the knotty problem of relating theory to practice by abandoning the theory altogether and giving students endless (often unguided) practice. The CNAA document (R3) mentioned above rightly states that 'It therefore becomes imperative that Institutions demonstrate that experience of the students in the school is not just experience per se, but that there is a carefully considered rationale which equips the student with aspects of what might have had to be omitted from the institutionally based content' and to verify those aspects which have been covered.

The alternative kinds of experience alluded to above – which can be used to gain knowledge about children's learning, develop skills and knowledge in presenting a subject, sample techniques and have sufficient time to evaluate them, learn some basic principles about group management and so on – are quite extensive. Most students go out on school visits to observe; many make child studies at school, home, college; serial and group practice is available in some cases. But several other opportunities have recently found their way into some courses. Examples are micro-observational teaching, testing individuals or groups of pupils, classroom observation and analysis, critical incident analysis, interviewing parents, tutor demonstrations, simulation exercises with small groups, paired observations. The use of data gathering or research of a theoretical kind is not included in this list. This kind of experience is probably best left until later in the career of a teacher. Research design and analysis require sophisticated knowledge and are somewhat time-consuming – and time is a scarce commodity in training. This does not exclude the possibility of conducting a small-scale study to test or develop a new or modified method of teaching. But rigorous, large-scale studies are so demanding of time and effort that they are impractical in training. The payoff for beginning students is also questionable. Findings from the limited samples researched by the inexperienced can only be tentative. Often a lot of hack work leads to very little information which is usable.

The role of trainees for a profession is a difficult one. They are caught between trying to do the work for which they are training as professionally as possible, while at the same time hoping to experiment and profit from the guidance of tutors and teachers. Admittedly, the block teaching practice timetable is not a full one and certain duties are not likely to come the student's way. It is rare to ask a student-teacher to meet parents to discuss the progress of children at a parent–teacher night, and few students know much about the practicalities of filling in school reports or making estimates of 'O' and 'A' level performance. Many other administrative duties, staff meetings and certain extra-curricular activities are not normally expected of a student, although many do volunteer. Any time which these exemptions might save is most frequently used in preparation and marking. Inevitably we have to use other means described above to enable students with tutors to engage in guided practice at teaching skills.

Evaluation of student effectiveness and the tutor's role

In trying to determine the essential qualities which students are expected to strive towards, perhaps the obvious place to start is the demands of the training institution and its tutors. What do they look for? What are the *actual* criteria used by tutors in judging teaching quality? Most training institutions have a standard diagnostic form to be completed by both tutors and the staff at the schools where students are placed. These inventories seem to me to be a logical source of information about the formative and summative evaluation of student effectiveness and performance.

In Chapter 6 on assessment, we will take a closer look at an assessment schedule characteristic of those used in training institutions. Here, we will look briefly at some major criteria employed in assessment and at the tutor's role. In Chapter 6, assessments are for convenience classified under four headings – pretask, formative, diagnostic and summative. Pretask assessment involves using a reliable test to estimate the basic

---

Table 1.1 *Some typical criteria used in formative and summative judgements of teaching competence.*

Preparation of schemes of work	These schemes cover the period of a practice and are usually drawn up during and after a visit to a school to discuss with teachers in the school the work to be done by the student. Students discover which class(es) are to be taken; age, sex, streamed or mixed ability; previous relevant work done by class in subjects to be taught; how many lessons and their duration; what subjects and which part of the syllabus; aims of the scheme; outline of methods; materials and resources available; any special organisational factors.
Preparation and planning of lessons	Clarity of aims and objectives – clear purposes and appropriate for the age, ability and background of the pupils; appropriate content suited to pupils' ability and the teaching methods; good selection of methods, materials.
Effective teaching	Arousing beginnings; clear presentation; good use of aids; pupil participation; control of class; communication skills; effective ending to the lesson.
Classroom management and organisation	Student/pupil rapport; personal relationships; effective management of the learning environment; safety; use of feedback.
Evaluation and assessment	Clear use of assessment methods; records of children's work; efficient feedback.
Professional qualities	Concern for professional standards; staffroom behaviour; reliable; dependable; seeking and using advice.

knowledge or skill which an individual brings to the learning. Actually, this is taken for granted in student selection, if the student has reached a sufficiently acceptable level in 'A' levels (for Bachelor's courses) or a degree (for PGCE courses).

DISCUSSION AND ANALYSIS ACTIVITIES

D1   As a group with a tutor, perhaps preceded by an essay on the subject, examine the most influential educational experiences that you had as pupils. As the theory course unfolds, many of these experiences will be explored for their psychological significance.

D2   Table 1.1 contains substantial portions of the syllabus you will cover in training. Look at the table and discuss with the tutors concerned how the criteria will fit into the syllabus. The professional training syllabus should be made explicit at the beginning of the student's course. Refer also to Chapter 6, Figures 6.1 and 6.2 and D7 (p. 118) for further material.

Formative assessment is more important in teaching practice. Tutors generally have a large number of general and specific criteria they use in trying to help a student forward. General criteria, for example, are preparation and planning for lessons, classroom performance, personal relationships, and assessment and evaluation techniques used by the student. Under each of these general headings, there are a great many specific issues of concern to the tutor. For a preliminary idea of these criteria see Table 1.1 (D2, p. 9). This book is devoted to an elaboration of these criteria and in Chapter 6 there are examples of actual proformas for formative, diagnostic and summative assessment. The first two are combined into one form, which is handed to the student (Figure 6.3). The summative assessment (Figure 6.4), used for the final school practice, is a compilation from all the relevant sources of information about a student's teaching performance. It is not only the tutor who contributes to this, but teachers in the school, other tutors who may be invited in, and occasionally an external examiner. External examiners sample the student population; they do not see every student. Sampling includes the exceptional (good and poor alike) as well as the competent.

TUTORS

Tutors in teacher education come in several forms! Some are 'method' specialists in particular subject areas and they often teach the main subject specialism as well as degree courses. Others specialise in educational and professional studies, most frequently from the behavioural sciences (psychology, sociology), philosophy or 'converts' from main subject areas who have usually taken educational studies as a further qualification. Students also have personal tutors and supervisory tutors for teaching practices, both plucked from the ranks of the above specialists.

A number of institutions now have staff development programmes, which include student questionnaires about the quality of the theory courses being taught by tutors. These are instructive from two points of view. First, they give the tutor important feedback on his or her teaching methods, and second, the questions on the forms give students an idea of the stress placed by the institution on various aspects of teaching. A sample is appended to this chapter (p. 14; also see D3, p. 14).

To shape up a coherent programme through training, it seems inevitable that personal and supervising tutors should work closely in guiding a student's progress. One purpose of teaching-practice visits is to offer assistance and advice, immediately after a lesson if possible, and these should be used to isolate problems and recommend some remedial course of action. The tutors' role is crucial in providing opportunities for additional formative or remedial experience. Tutors have to be inventive in finding different ways in which to expose students to opportunities for practice. As there is no one route to effective teaching, the variety of methods available should be exploited to the full. Students' strengths and weaknesses arise from an amalgam of past experience and the college courses. The weaknesses sometimes take a lot of removing. One of the tutors' tasks is to find methods which are sufficiently potent to have an effect. Some ideas are listed below.

THE SCHOOL

The training of teachers is heavily dependent on the co-operation of schools. The head teacher, teachers and pupils devote time and effort to help in the process. Every effort should be made to make the school involvement profitable for all concerned. At all costs avoid creating the impression that the schools are being 'used' to satisfy the training institution's needs. Over the years very good relationships are built up between tutors and the schools. Sometimes this involves the tutor, and teachers and students in many forms of group teaching enterprises.

It should be borne in mind that most forms of co-operation which involve teachers and pupils have some disruptive influence, and we should be thankful that schools are so willing and able to give help and advice to student-teachers. We should capitalise on the wealth of valuable experience they offer with the least imposition to the school system.

ALTERNATIVE OPPORTUNITIES FOR FORMATIVE PRACTICE

Trying out ideas, correcting faulty strategies, finding time to reflect on good or poor procedures cannot, and *should not*, be left to the final stages of school practice. Other occasions mentioned above have to be found when such analytical and reflective methods can be pursued, without disrupting the school system. Alternative opportunities for formative work include the following (see D4, p. 14).

School observation visits

These usually take place early on in training – sometimes before joining a training course. If this happens, it is essential for the training institution to give clear guidance to the host school and the student as to what is expected. A report from the school should be sought. Bear in mind what is realistic when a potential student has not even started a course.

Serial practice

Some institutions organise a regular half-day or day a week over an extended period. These can frequently be used for exploratory study and not just more of the same each week.

Child studies

These are very important. It is not surprising to find many students who welcome the prospect of studying child behaviour in some depth. It is not an activity we normally engage in and it can be most illuminating. The tutor has to ensure that the studies do not get out of hand. There is so much to look at, guidance is needed. One possibility is to break down the study into areas of interest and have one student look at one area. An observation manual can then be compiled from the students' observations.

In some cases, there is objective 'bird watching' observation (this is *not* an easy task – useful observation requires skills which have to be learned). In others, the student may become involved in a short programme with the child. Testing groups of children or individuals is sometimes possible, but administering, scoring and analysing test material has to be well organised and overseen.

In all the above activities, little should be taken for granted as far as student knowledge is concerned. All observation requires careful monitoring and tuition.

Tutor and teacher demonstration lessons

At one time this was a very common method of getting across some of the basic principles of classroom activity, and it still has a place. It is not infrequent to find a tutor and a small group of students engaged in a joint teaching session with a class, sharing the tasks and pooling the experiences. Students are often allowed to sit in on teachers' lessons when on practice. This should be a splendid opportunity for observing experience in action.

Microteaching

This is now quite popular in training institutions. A fragment of the teaching process is singled out and captured on video. It could be a student or a tutor demonstrating over a fairly short period (10 to 15 minutes) some specific aspects of teaching such as questioning, non-verbal cues, lesson introduction or closure, etc. Playback for those who have never seen themselves teach is sometimes a nasty shock! We begin to see ourselves as others see us. Just occasionally the shock is so great that a person becomes 'deskilled', i.e. they become so aware of their faults that they freeze up on future occasions. Fortunately this is rare.

Capturing on tape the kinds of topics which lend themselves to micro-technique (and not all topics do) enables a very useful library to be built up which can be drawn on when required.

Evaluation sheets are sometimes prepared and completed by the tutor for the benefit of the student (Table 1.2). Tutors have to be tactful and sensitive in analysing student performance to avoid the effects of deskilling, i.e. demoralising students to the point where they begin to lose the skills they already possess.

Table 1.2 *Trainee evaluation checklist.* Lesson: techniques of managing disruptive behaviour in the classroom.

Specified skill tasks	Check satisfactory performance
1. Systematically ignores attention-getting mechanisms of a non-serious nature	☐
2. Communicates non-verbal signals of disapproval to learner	☐
3. Uses physical contact or proximity to assist learners in behaviour control	☐
4. Helps learner with frustrating work	☐
5. Changes task when work is clearly causing continued frustration	☐
6. Uses humour to relieve tension (if appropriate)	☐
7. Uses 'change of scene' to avoid outburst	☐
8. If physical restraint is necessary, uses minimal force necessary – and without emotional-laden comment	☐

Supervisor's comments:

From R.N. Jensen, *Microteaching*, p. 45, Charles C. Thomas, Springfield, Illinois, 1974. Reproduced with permission.

Classroom observation

Classroom observation of a more specific nature than the school observation visit mentioned above can be very valuable. Critical incidents in the life of the classroom can be pinpointed and observed systematically using standard observation schedules. Teacher–pupil interaction, teacher language, pupil language, class management, pupil deviance can be recorded and scrutinised afterwards for content of a useful kind. Again, such systematic obervations are not easy and require careful preparation. For an example of an observation schedule, see Wragg, or Walker and Adelman (R4).

Other opportunities

Other opportunities for practice or observation include the following: (a) Simulation – students act as pupils and a lesson is given to them by a student. 'Lecturettes' constitute a popular method used in short courses introducing, for example, new university lecturers to the mysteries of teaching. The lecturettes are taped and played back for analysis by other lecturers. (b) Students sometimes teach in pairs rather than singly and use each other as a source of information about obvious flaws in teaching methods. (c) RAP (radio-assisted practice) can also be used; it is a radio means of communicating with a student during the process of teaching. First reactions are that when a student hears a voice through the receiver (like a hearing aid in one ear), (s)he will be put off. The evidence so far suggests that this is *not* the case. To quote the originators (Smith and Tomlinson, R5):

> RAP . . . allows unobtrusive communication from tutor to trainee teacher during actual teaching activity . . . The findings of studies of the use of RAP with the authors and a small number of B.Ed. and PGCE students on school practice confirm the considerable power of the technique and the need for tutor and student preparation for effective RAP use.

There are other devices used by tutors to extend the experience of students. As we move into a period when greater thought will be given to ways of enhancing training programmes, most, if not all, of the above strategies will be taken on board.

DISCUSSION AND ANALYSIS ACTIVITIES

D3   Both tutors and students at a very early stage in the course might benefit from a discussion about the sample questionnaire reproduced in the appendix to this chapter (p. 14). The questionnaire gives some good suggestions for the student when he or she is on teaching practice.

D4   Take each of the alternative opportunities offered, i.e. school observation visit, serial practice, child studies, tutor demonstrations, microteaching, classroom observation and other opportunities, and explore the possibilities they offer for additional practice.

Appendix

Student Feedback Questionnaire[1]

This questionnaire is designed to help your tutor to get information about student reaction to the part of the course you are just completing.

This information will help to improve the course for the benefit of future course members.

The term UNIT in the questionnaire refers to the part of the course you are just completing. If you are not sure exactly what it is you are being asked to comment on, ask the lecturer before you start.

Try to be as objective in your replies as possible. Do not let your overall reaction to the course (either favourable or unfavourable) influence specific replies to particular questions.

Do not put either your name or the name of any of your tutors on the questionnaire. The replies will be most useful if they are entirely anonymous.

Part 1: General impact of the unit

Place a ✔ in the
appropriate box

1. How DIFFICULT did you find the unit?
   - 1 Very difficult
   - 2 Fairly difficult
   - 3 Just right
   - 4 Fairly easy
   - 5 Very easy

2. How INTERESTING did you find the unit?
   - 1 Very interesting
   - 2 Fairly interesting
   - 3 Not very interesting
   - 4 Of no interest at all

3. Was enough TIME allocated for the amount of work involved?
   - 1 Not enough time
   - 2 Just right
   - 3 Too much time

4. To what extent have you UNDERSTOOD the unit?
   - 1 Thoroughly
   - 2 Fairly well
   - 3 Partially
   - 4 Hardly at all

5. To what extent were you clear about the AIMS of the unit?
   - 1 Quite clear
   - 2 Partially clear
   - 3 Not clear at all

6. How VALUABLE have you found the unit?
   1 Very valuable
   2 Fairly valuable
   3 Not very valuable
   4 Hardly any value

7. How SATISFIED are you with this unit?
   1 Highly satisfied
   2 Quite satisfied
   3 Not very satisfied
   4 Very dissatisfied

Part 2: Teaching strategies and techniques

How useful have you found the following teaching strategies and techniques in helping you to achieve the objectives of the unit?

Please respond as follows by putting a ring around the response you choose:

Very useful	3
Fairly useful	2
Not very useful	1
Of no use	0
Not included in this unit – probably not relevant to the material	–
Not included in this unit – might have been useful if included	+

	No use	Not very useful	Fairly useful	Very useful	
Lectures	–	+	0	1	2	3
Seminars, discussion groups, etc.	–	+	0	1	2	3
Tutorials	–	+	0	1	2	3
Practical classes	–	+	0	1	2	3
Private study	–	+	0	1	2	3
Reading lists	–	+	0	1	2	3
Set books	–	+	0	1	2	3
Other library books	–	+	0	1	2	3
Handouts	–	+	0	1	2	3
Dictated notes	–	+	0	1	2	3
Demonstrations	–	+	0	1	2	3

		No use	Not very useful	Fairly useful	Very useful
Films, TV, etc.	− +	0	1	2	3
Blackboard summaries and illustrations	− +	0	1	2	3
Projects	− +	0	1	2	3
Problems...	− +	0	1	2	3
Case studies, simulations, etc.......................	− +	0	1	2	3
Tests...	− +	0	1	2	3
Exercises done in class	− +	0	1	2	3
Exercises done in private study	− +	0	1	2	3

Part 3: The teacher

Do you agree or disagree with the following statements? Indicate the level of your agreement by circling a number in the left hand margin as follows:

Strongly agree 4
Agree 3
Neither agree nor disagree....................2
Disagree..1
Strongly disagree 0

The lecturer −

Neither agree nor disagree		Strongly agree	
1	2	3	4	Is clear and understandable in his or her explanations
1	2	3	4	Presents material in a well-organised way
1	2	3	4	Gives a good factual coverage of the subject matter
1	2	3	4	Identifies and stresses important aspects
1	2	3	4	Writes legibly on the blackboard or projector
1	2	3	4	Can be clearly heard
1	2	3	4	Adjusts his or her pace to the needs of the class
1	2	3	4	Stimulates students to think independently
1	2	3	4	Is sensitive to the feelings and problems of individual students
1	2	3	4	Encourages students to ask questions
1	2	3	4	Answers questions satisfactorily
1	2	3	4	Encourages students to express their own views

Neither agree nor disagree

Strongly agree

1	2	3	4	Sets interesting and worthwhile tests and exercises
1	2	3	4	Makes constructive and helpful comments on written work and practical tasks
1	2	3	4	Is enthusiastic about his or her subject
1	2	3	4	Points out the links between his or her subjects and related subjects
1	2	3	4	Tries to create links between various parts of the course, e.g. between lectures and laboratory exercises
1	2	3	4	Shows the relevance of his or her subject to the work you expect to do when you qualify
1	2	3	4	Is approachable
1	2	3	4	Has a good sense of humour

REFERENCES

R1 D. Child, *Psychology and the Teacher*, Holt, Rinehart and Winston, Eastbourne, 4th Edn, 1986.

R2 R.W. Tyler, *Basic Principles of Curriculum and Instruction*, University of Chicago Press, Chicago, 1949.

R3 Council for National Academic Awards, *Perspectives on Postgraduate Initial Training. The CNAA validated PGCE*, CNAA, London, 1984.

R4 E.C. Wragg (Ed.), *Classroom Teaching Skills*, Croom Helm, London, 1984, pp. 209–219. R. Walker and C. Adelman, *A Guide to Classroom Observation*, Methuen, London, 1975.

R5 R. Smith and P. Tomlinson, 'RAP: radio-assisted practice. Preliminary investigations of a new technique in teacher education', *Journal of Education for Teaching*, **10**, 119–134 (1984).

2

Knowledge of the Subjects and the Learners

At the beginning of a career in teaching there is much essential knowledge needed about teaching the subjects of the curriculum and those being taught. For example, at the start of any academic year, new pupils are inherited from other teachers and/or other schools. In infant and primary (and some middle) schools, the year usually begins with a completely new set of faces – each one with a unique history of educational opportunities and deficiencies. In secondary schools, the faces are sometimes new and sometimes carry over from previous years. Getting to know the background of each pupil is a tremendous, sometimes slow, but necessary task in order to become informed and continue the process of building up a profile of the pupil. School records are obviously a vital source of information in this process.

In this chapter, we shall look at two aspects of this important activity of obtaining background knowledge. The first, dealt with briefly because it is of more concern to subject specialists than psychologists, is the *basic knowledge of the subject or subjects* you are teaching (the syllabus and how it fits into what has gone before), in order to ensure that the levels are suitable and appropriate for the competence of the pupils. The second is *knowledge of the new children* entering your class(es) in terms of previous educational exposure (cognitive entry characteristics).

THE SUBJECT(S)

Teaching is now an all-graduate-entry profession and all students study some academic subjects of their own choosing to an advanced stage. Some of these subjects will be relevant to the student's subsequent teaching choices, particularly specialist teachers in secondary or primary education. In infant, junior and lower middle school, the specialist is less in evidence – only in such subjects as music, PE, some crafts and very occasionally in science do we find a specialist on the staff who does most of the teaching in that subject area. The teacher of junior age-ranges is required to have a wide knowledge base at a less advanced level for work in the schools, although specialist knowledge is sometimes called upon and welcomed in the primary schools. Some schools deliberately set up specialist groups to capitalise on the expertise and to act as a source of advice to other teachers.

Ideas about the content, sequencing, amount suitable for a lesson, level of concepts attainable by a given class are essential. One soon loses sight of the capacities of others in pursuing one's own interests in a subject. Some mathematics and science teachers, for example, become renowned for their ability to baffle pupils with their knowledge of a subject. They treat the subjects in such a high-powered way, failing to appreciate the problems experienced by others in understanding basic concepts. 'I can't understand why the pupils don't understand . . . It's so easy.' The skill of converting complex ideas into simple presentations which learners can follow is one to be developed.

Details of overall syllabuses are occasionally laid down by a school and always by examining bodies, and in this case the teacher does not have too much room for manoeuvre. Further down the system there can be tremendous latitude in the content of the curriculum. A teacher in those circumstances has to know how to set about choosing an appropriate syllabus for a particular age and ability range. Much has been written about this as an outcome of curriculum development projects – many, for instance, instigated by what used to be known as the Schools Council, which was set up in the 1960s to advise schools about curricula (Barnes, R1). An appendix to this chapter (p. 36) contains a comprehensive list of projects undertaken for the Schools Council.

It is not appropriate in this text to look in detail at particular subjects. The major sources of help and guidance are the *method* sessions, which form part of the teacher-training programme, and your discussions with experienced teachers in your special field. In *PAT* (R2), illustrations are given of particular problems in certain subject areas for which psychology might have some advice. Also, for an overall view of curriculum planning, see Chapter 16 in *PAT*.

ENTRY CHARACTERISTICS OF THE LEARNER

The history of a learner, both cognitive and affective, has much to do with his or her present performance in a relevant area. The term *entry characteristics* (or *behaviours*) is used in the American literature (Bloom, R3) and means those aspects of a child's academic and personal history which are likely to influence performance on the task proposed for the lesson (see also *PAT*, R4). These characteristics will be dealt with under two headings, *cognitive* and *affective*. Before dealing with them in any detail, however, it should be mentioned that some psychologists divide the entry characteristics into static (or unalterable) predispositions, such as measured intelligence and personality, and *alterable* predispositions, any factor which can be influenced by the teacher, such as reading comprehension, study skills and so forth. The reason measured intelligence and personality are regarded as unalterable is part and parcel of their definition. By definition, these two qualities are not expected to fluctuate wildly from time to time for any one person. Such variation would render the measures unreliable. Therefore, the information they provide is snap-shot, for the most part unchangeable, but predictive. For the teacher, the alterable factors – the ones over which she or he has some control – are the most interesting. Measures of intelligence or personality would provide background information indicating potential (R5).

COGNITIVE ENTRY CHARACTERISTICS

By cognitive entry characteristics (R4) is meant those intellectual attributes which a person brings to a task resulting from previous experience. A pupil's previous learning, development and abilities are bound to be influential prerequisites in a given learning task. It would be difficult (some say impossible) to think of a learning task we offer in school that does not require some prerequisite learning.

The sorts of influence we shall consider here are early home experience, curriculum experiences at school prior to the task, communication skills (particularly verbal and numerical), intellectual abilities, stage of development and previous performance.

Home experience

Home educational experiences of children do play a part in later performance. Douglas, Ross and Simpson (R6) showed that home influences were important throughout school life, but were especially potent in the *pre-school* years and at school-leaving age. In the present context, the pre-school years are especially significant. In a summary of the research into the effect of early parental involvement, Smith (R7) shows that, despite the adverse findings from early research such as *Head Start* in America (R8), most of the more recent work gives positive, hopeful results (D1, p. 24). Smith concludes:

> both American and British evidence shows clearly that programmes involving parents with their children can affect both parents' confidence and competence and their children's development. Secondly, the crucial component seems to be the parents' role as educators of their children, with active participation. Thirdly, if the process of adult–child interaction is essentially one of mutual responsiveness, with parent and child mutually reinforcing each other, then the question is how to initiate and maintain this as a positive cycle for the developing child. Fourthly, a possible hypothesis from Lazar and Darlington's [R9] findings is the strength and continuity of this mutual responsiveness, once established, throughout the child's school career. Fifthly, the process of parental participation is essentially to do with adult education: how and where adults learn *how to assist their children in the pre-school years*. [my italics: R7] [D2, p. 24].

The longitudinal research of Douglas, Ross and Simpson (R6) and the National Children's Bureau (Essen and Wedge, R10) and the evidence collected for the Plowden Report on children and their primary schools (Peaker, R11) are consistent in pointing to certain influences linking children's educational achievement and parental attitudes and expectations (the 'educational climate' at home). The findings can be summarised as possible pieces of advice to parents, when teachers are discussing a pupil's progress.

(a)   Become actively involved in the state education of your child – visit the school when necessary, seek advice, be keen to show you want your children to attain well, obtain good exam results and, if possible, stay on at school.

(b)   Don't hesitate to see the teacher when necessary.

(c)   Fathers should show an interest as well as mothers.

(d)   The time spent by mothers on educationally valuable topics seems to be proportional in some cases to the child's school performance.

(e)   There is a link between the literacy and literary interests of parents and the successs of children (books in the home, library membership).

Examples of disadvantage can be found in *PAT* (R12); see also P1 (p. 24).

One of the weaknesses of this line of research was that it gave a description of the situation, but said nothing about how one might improve the lot of those least fortunate. The role of the nursery and playgroup is of some significance here (P2, p. 24).

However, Lazar and Darlington (R9) have shown that early pre-school intervention does affect school performance. Attitudes towards school achievement were also affected (for more detail see *PAT*, R13). These are, in fact, long-term effects both on educational and attitudinal aspects, and they are both related to improved academic performance. The researchers suggest that the best effects are probably cyclical – mutual reinforcement between parents and child: parents encourage and help their child → and the child does well → parental interest and encouragement grows → and the spiral of mutual reinforcement continues.

Several researchers have taken the additional step of introducing parents to educational training programmes at home (or possibly at evening classes). These programmes of systematic parental involvement (R14) were successful in improving the children's development (compared with a control group), and *this lasted throughout and beyond school years*. This question of the permanence of early training is quite critical, because the teacher needs to know how lasting the early accomplishments of pupils will be, if they have their origins in home tuition. The conclusion is significant for teachers of younger children. It seems (R7, for a summary) that systematic advice to parents encouraging them to be 'educators' without formal training can be of value in both the parents' attitudes to their children's progress and in improving their children's school performance. The major problem one has to guard against is the well-meaning amateur whose interventions in the education of his/her children could do irreparable damage.

Early curriculum experiences

One of the first tasks of a student or beginning teacher is to discover what the children have already covered in previous lessons by others, before deciding on the next task. Some topics are sequential, such as mathematics and science, and this should help in the process of discovering the point in the sequence already reached *and* those parts omitted from the sequence. Discovering what children have done in other subjects can be more problematic, and advice from the training institution and experienced teachers is especially helpful in building up some progressive timetable of work.

Discovering the stage reached by pupils whom you have just met for the first time is very difficult. Sometimes in the primary school information is passed on from teacher to teacher (P3, p. 25). Further up the system it becomes harder to discover the stage reached, unless there is an examination syllabus being worked through or the school has a set

---

PRACTICE AND OBSERVATION ACTIVITIES

P1   Discuss with a relative or friend with pre-school children the issues raised in (a) to (e) (p. 22). It is not feasible to conduct a systematic research into these, but you could make some observations about the various ways in which the parents with whom you speak take an active interest in the educational development of their child and the extent to which they try to achieve this. What provision do they make at home (toys, games, parent–child interaction such as reading or play with an educational outcome)?

P2   If an opportunity arises, see if a small group can visit a play group, crèche or nursery with a tutor. Note the organisation, timetable, 'syllabus', what hangs on the wall, relationships, and so on.

DISCUSSION AND ANALYSIS ACTIVITIES

D1   We live in hope that if only we knew the secret, we could accelerate the intellectual development of our children. Read up and discuss the various research studies on this topic. You will find *PAT*, Chapters 8 and 12 a useful starting point for references on compensatory education, *Head Start*, etc.

D2   Discuss the following issues: What role has the teacher in encouraging parents to be 'educators' of their own children during their school years? Can teachers help in providing adult education advice for parents of pre-school children? What home background factors does the teacher need to know about in order to help the parent of the early school-age child?

---

syllabus. The first year entry in a school is especially hazardous, because the children often come from different schools. Some skills are taken on trust. For example, pupils fresh into a comprehensive school at the age of 11 might all be expected to cope with the four rules of number. But with many aspects of the work finding the stage reached could well resolve itself into trial and error, discovering bit by bit the areas of weakness or neglect. What is even more difficult to cope with is how much of his/her previous experience and knowledge the pupil can remember in order to cope with existing tasks. Knowledge that a part of a syllabus has been covered previously is not enough; one has to discover how much is remembered using various kinds of assessment. Repetition, revision, overlapping curriculum areas are essential – provided they are not overdone to the point of boredom.

Keeping a close eye on systematic errors can be rewarding (see *PAT*, R15). Errors give clues to work which has been forgotten, not done, badly taught, ill-digested, too difficult and so on. Error analysis for trends and some careful questioning of children can uncover sources of difficulties and provide material for subsequent lessons (D3, p. 25). Such entry knowledge is vital.

PRACTICE AND OBSERVATION ACTIVITIES

P3 While on observation at a school, ask the teachers how they obtain information about the work covered in previous classes. What is the record card system? Are there discussions with teachers in other schools where appropriate?

DISCUSSION AND ANALYSIS ACTIVITIES

D3 Error analysis can be an important source of information about children's problems. Read the accounts of error analysis provided by the Department of Education and Science through the work of the Assessment of Performance Unit (APU).

Communication skills

School life – indeed all life – is enriched and dependent on communication. Without basic skills in different modes of communication, school life is impossible. Modes of communication such as written and spoken language, number, music, body movement, painting have to be mastered before conventional subjects can proceed. The two most widely used modes are verbal and numerical.

Verbal skills

Our educational system is very 'wordy'. We depend heavily on verbal comprehension. Tests of school achievement frequently include some measure of verbal ability and comprehension. Research has shown a correlation between reading comprehension and achievement in other subjects, including mathematics (this correlation is less apparent with some aspects of science, but there is still a positive relationship, because one cannot even read and understand questions in science without some verbal facility).

The clear conclusion from research in this field (see R3 for a summary) is that reading comprehension is an essential prerequisite for later learning in school work. Even if the teacher's skills have faltered in presenting a topic, the pupil with adequate reading skills can go away and learn for him or herself.

Reading looms very large in the syllabus of primary schools. At secondary level, teachers also need to be vigilant in ensuring that every opportunity is given to pupils for reading comprehension. Lesson planning should from time to time include this element quite deliberately.

There are standardised tests of reading comprehension, such as NFER reading tests A and AD, which may be necessary at the beginning of the infant and early primary-school years with a new class. Actually, such a test at the beginning of a secondary-school career would be quite enlightening! It is certainly wise in the junior years to have a clear idea of the level of competence in reading as a new class begins.

Children's skills in using language have been looked at by Tough (refer to *PAT*, R16). She concludes that:

> The essential experience for promoting the development and use of language appears to be the talk into which a child is drawn, and which helps the child to structure and set value on his experiences, and think about them in certain ways ... Teachers of young children might play a crucial role in influencing children's development and use of language if they were aware of the kind of help needed by each child and were able to provide appropriate experiences for all the children in the class. [Tough, R17]

See the *Schools Council's Skills in Early Childhood Project* (R18).

Numerical skills

Like language acquisition and development, quantitative skills depend on the exposures and cumulative experiences of early life. Evidence seems to show that pre-school children are not given anything like the same exposure to number concepts as language. The bridges to number understanding necessary in nursery school or reception classes are much harder to build.

Most analyses of the development of number skills assume a gradual hierarchical build-up of concepts with ever-increasing complexity. There is a considerable literature on mathematical (and scientific) developmental frameworks, which will be considered by students in their method sessions, if they are going to teach the subject at primary or secondary level. The two most popular approaches are those involving stratification of skills (such as Gagné's approach, R19) and those describing concept development, usually as a function of intellectual age (Piaget's approach, R19). A study of these alongside the syllabus recommendations and knowledge learned about your children's competences is an obvious requirement in lesson planning.

As mentioned above, the role of early home and school experiences is important in the development of quantitative skills. There is much evidence to show a positive correlation between early arithmetic performance and later competence. Home opportunities have a powerful effect on later performance, and earlier skills, such as arithmetical manipulation, seem to be a necessary prerequisite for more advanced activities like algebra (D4, p. 27). Bloom (R3) summarises the research evidence thus:

> In *arithmetic*, the *knowledge about numbers* acquired earlier appears to be one of the consistent predictors of achievement in 1st grade arithmetic. While this does not appear to fully satisfy our requirements or necessary prerequisite learning (any more than prior knowledge of the alphabet for reading), it is a consistent predictor of later arithmetic achievement. We believe that elemental notions about quantitative relations are developed in pre-school experiences (e.g. older than, time, number of eyes, number of siblings, bigger than) and that some knowledge of numbers is a crude but useful symptom of the extent and quality of these experiences. [p. 45]

DISCUSSION AND ANALYSIS ACTIVITIES

D4   It is important to analyse your chosen subject(s) in terms of current theories of development and skill stratification.
In the method sessions, keep an eye open for all the references you can find on this topic.

Intellectual abilities

Standardised tests of various intellectual abilities in verbal, numerical and spatial form are still widely used as *predictors* of performance in school achievement. Some areas of the country still operate the 11 + examination, and many primary and secondary schools occasionally test their children for diagnostic purposes (on transfer or if a child does not seem to be achieving as well as expected). Educational psychologists also use them (P4, p. 28).

For the teacher, a knowledge of a child's potential is obviously important. Measures of intellectual ability, however, can only give a rough idea of expectations; they say nothing about how one might tackle deficiencies. They give us a clue as to how much of a problem we have, but not how to remedy it! By definition, the standardised scores of ability are not supposed to vary much for any one person and that is why they are regarded by some psychologists as static and unalterable (D5, p. 28).

PRACTICE AND OBSERVATION ACTIVITIES

P4   On any visit to a school, discover the use, if any, which is made of standardised intelligence tests. Note the tests in use. Discuss the use made of the scores with teachers.

DISCUSSION AND ANALYSIS ACTIVITIES

D5   Chapter 9 in *PAT* is devoted to a discussion of intelligence. In the Enquiry and Discussion section at the end of that chapter there are several questions which ought to be raised in tutorials. Particularly practical issues are questions in (b), (g) and (h). Read also *PAT*, Chapter 9, pp. 203–212.

Stage of development

One extreme view is that you can teach anybody anything, barring the cogenitally unfortunate with natural deficiencies, given sufficient time and appropriately directed effort. In the real educational world, time is not limitless and effort has to be shared amongst many children. In this imperfect world we have to look for short-cuts.

One well-established short-cut is the developmental school of thought which gives descriptions of children's competence at different ages or stages. These are sometimes chronological ages, but they may be intellectual (e.g. mental age, 'reading age') (see R20). Reservations are expressed about using these criteria, because the level of development of individuals varies widely between them and fluctuates in its progress with any one person – sometimes a steady growth, sometimes a spurt, sometimes things seem to stagnate or even decline. Also, if one sticks too rigidly to the idea of a fixed age–stage theory, it tends to discourage attempts to accelerate the process of learning.

For a teacher, a 'stages of development' approach is convenient. It gives a base-line of expectations from which to make judgements about what might come next. It gives a yardstick by which to assess the quality of the entry characteristics and places these in perspective. Without some assumptions as to what we can reasonably expect at a given age, especially with large classes, where some parts of the lesson might involve a large group or the whole class, life for teachers would become unmanageable.

In estimating and applying the entry qualities of pupils, student-teachers and teachers will find these descriptive accounts of children's development in particular fields very helpful (D6).

DISCUSSION AND ANALYSIS ACTIVITIES

D6 There are a number of texts on the market dealing with child development such as Mussen, Conger, Kagan and Huston; or primers by Sylva and Lunt; or Branthwaite and Rogers (R21). It is inevitable that your tutorial group in education will regularly return to this topic. You need to build up a working file on the subject of child development.

Previous performance

It should not come as a surprise to readers that one of the clearest predictors of present performance in school is past performance in school. Bloom (R3) sets great store by the observation and concludes that longitudinal studies of achievement show correlations between grade 2 and grade 12 (8-year-olds and 18-year-olds) of $+0.60$, between grade 6 and 12 of $+0.78$ and between grade 10 and 12 of $+0.90$. These are high correlations and significant for the sample sizes used. There also seems to be increasing stability of achievement with increasing age. The same does not seem to hold true when 'A' level results are compared with degree results, but this may depend on the comparability of the subjects being studied and the differences in the styles of teaching, examining and concept complexity between sixth-form and university or polytechnic courses (P5, D7, p. 30).

These correlations point to the significance and importance of obtaining for a new set of children the previous scholastic records. However, it is most important *not* to allow this knowledge to be the start of a self-fulfilling prophecy (*PAT*, pp. 52–54) in which pupils perform only as well (or as badly) as you speculate.

PRACTICE AND OBSERVATION ACTIVITIES

P5   There are certain intelligence and standardised tests which teachers can use. If the opportunity presents itself for you to be involved – even if only as an observer – when children are being tested, don't miss it. Some tutors might be involved in a testing programme. Perhaps you could join in.

DISCUSSION AND ANALYSIS ACTIVITIES

D7   The use of standardised tests as part of classroom practice is very important. You should be encouraged to inspect as many as you can which are relevant to your subject. These need to be discussed in tutorials – their strengths and limitations. Cross-reference to *PAT*, Chapter 14, on standardised tests will give you other reference material.

AFFECTIVE ENTRY CHARACTERISTICS

By *affective entry characteristics* is meant those individual differences in self-concept of ability, effects of success or failure, motivation and interest, personality, that have an impact on academic achievement. Persistent failure (for whatever reasons), a person with a self-image dogged by pessimism about achievement, someone lacking in interest or motivation, an over-anxious or butterfly mind are all likely to lead to lowered performance. Such influences may be present at the outset of a lesson and will probably reduce the quality and quantity of work done – affective factors therefore account for some of the variation in subsequent academic achievement.

Apart from some of the personality characteristics which are regarded as stable in their appearance, the other variables mentioned above are capable of coming under the influence and control of the teacher. They are alterable. It seems that only after a long, persistent and consistent history of failure or damaged self-image, or prolonged boredom and lack of interest do the affective factors become almost impervious to beneficial teacher influences. But this kind of information is clearly important as background to decisions which the teacher might make in dealing with particular children.

The effect of success and failure

Feedback effects

Pupils – as with students on teacher-training courses – interpret the feedback they receive from others and use this feedback to evaluate their competence and worth. Regular success is likely to build up confidence. Regular failure is likely to lead to abandoning a subject or just not making the effort.

Reactions to success or failure are discussed in *PAT* (R22). Reactions to failure are not always adverse, if failure is not a persistent feature of feedback. Lack of effort (for example, where a pupil did not revise for a test and did badly in it) may not necessarily lead to an adverse reaction the next time a test is given. It is more likely to lead to more effort. Lack of understanding or ability to cope with the level of concepts being dealt with is much more likely to depress future performance (P6, p. 32).

Subject interest

There is evidence to show a positive correlation between a pupil's interest in a subject and the level of achievement in that subject. Whether the interest grows as a result of high achievement or achievement increases a pupil's interest is still a matter for debate and investigation. Possibly the effect is cyclical, and both interest and achievement grow together, i.e. are mutually enhancing.

School and learning

Some children develop a dislike of school and all it stands for. There is evidence that the degree of liking for school and achievement are related (e.g. Bloom, R3). On entry to school, children have only a vague idea of the demands it will make. They are, understandably, apprehensive of what it holds in store for them. Parents' and teachers' attitudes to school play an important part in forming the opinions held by pupils. Pupils' successes and failures in adjusting to school life – not just academic work as indicated above, but socially as well – are of significance (P7, p. 32).

PRACTICE AND OBSERVATION ACTIVITIES

P6   Refer to *PAT*, Chapter 3, pp. 48–54 and other relevant literature recommended. Determine ways in which you might try to discover the sources of failure in a pupil in a particular subject of interest to you. Get your tutor's approval, and the co-operation of a school to try out your ideas with a few children who are failing.

P7   There are a number of 'interest' scales available – attitudes to school, particular subjects, teachers and so forth. Tutors should make these available and a scheme should be worked out so that the student can ask two or three pupils (in school or perhaps relatives or friends) about their likes and dislikes – and why! For ideas, see Cohen (R23).

Academic self-concept

As well as attitudes to the subject of study and school learning, we develop 'attitudes' to ourselves as learners. We are ever watchful about what other people think of our performance, and the image we create of ourselves is dependent on this feedback. It is our own perceptions of how others see us which provide the foundation stones for our academic self-image.

Positive correlations have been found between measures of self-concept of ability and achievement. Some studies (summarised in Bloom, R3) have shown self-concept to be more strongly linked with achievement than the other affective variables mentioned above (P8).

PRACTICE AND OBSERVATION ACTIVITIES

P8   There are a number of cross-references to *PAT* on the subject of academic self-concept. See particularly Chapter 3, pp. 52–54 and Chapter 11, pp. 243–245. Questions from the Brookover test of academic self-concept should prove useful. For these, look at Cohen's book (R23).

Motivation and interest

Some aspects of motivation and interest of pupils in class have already been examined above. We looked at the home as a source of encouragement and as giving a basic grounding in the kinds of activities which are rewarded by the educational system; earlier school experiences may have developed or killed interest in particular subjects or in the process of education itself; the extrinsic and intrinsic reward systems of the school may enhance or inhibit the interests of pupils; academic self-concept may depress or enliven a child's approach to learning. In all these instances, the level of motivation would affect performance.

In *PAT* (R24), evidence was presented on the influence of the 'need for achievement' and 'fear of failure' and on the levels of aspiration of school children and their effects on performance. Some investigation of these factors is absolutely essential in relation to your own pupils. No knowledge of their interests and 'turn-offs' can get in the way of effective planning for anticipating problems, designing counter-measures and channelling a pupil's energies in the directions required (P9 and P10).

PRACTICE AND OBSERVATION ACTIVITIES

P9 On school observation, carefully note those activities which children in particular age-groups enjoy. Can these be turned to good effect in class? What criteria have you used for detecting interest and enthusiasm amongst children? Discuss with your tutors whether these are valid criteria. Observe children at play and note the differences according to age. Can these observations be used to good effect in the classroom? Where do teachers draw the line between play and work?

P10 Note the use made by teachers of incentives. Compare the relative merits of incentives in particular age-groups and ability ranges.

Personality

There is some disagreement among psychologists as to whether personality is more or less stable and fixed in the earlier years of life, or whether it is capable of being manipulated or modified substantially enough to affect school performance. In general, personality is regarded as a fairly stable set of attributes which are only likely to be changed following some traumatic experience. Those who believe that it is largely a stable set of attributes would question the value of a detailed knowledge of personality and a description that would help to account for any unusual or useful characteristics related to academic achievement.

In the chapter on personality in *PAT* (Chapter 11), a middle position was taken. We do know that anxiety, fear, extravert/introvert characteristics can be related to school performance. Too much anxiety has damaging effects on performance – what can be done to control levels of anxiety in the classroom? What generates anxiety in children at different ages? What creates fear in pupils and can it be controlled? Is it possible to tailor teaching methods to allow for personality differences in children, e.g. pace, variation in the kinds of materials presented, bookish, pictorial or practical presentations? (P11).

PRACTICE AND OBSERVATION ACTIVITIES

P11   On observation or practice, ask teachers how they control levels of anxiety in the classroom, what generates anxiety in children (at different ages) and fear of failure? Can teaching methods be tailored to suit personality differences in children – how do teachers tackle this? Can one vary the pace, materials presented, make some approaches for some children more 'bookish', pictorial or practical?

REFERENCES

R1   D. Barnes, *Practical Curriculum Study*, Routledge and Kegan Paul, London, 1982, Chapter 4.

R2   Some advances in certain school subject areas: *PAT*, Chapter 7, pp. 156–157.

R3   B. S. Bloom, *Human Characteristics and School Learning*, McGraw-Hill, New York, 1976.

R4   Entry characteristics: *PAT*, Chapter 5, pp. 107–109.

R5   Definitions and measures of intelligence: *PAT*, Chapter 9; and personality: Chapter 11.

R6   J. W. B. Douglas, J. M. Ross and H. R. Simpson, *All our Future: a Longitudinal Study of Secondary Education*, Davies, London, 1968. *PAT*, Chapter 9, pp. 208–209.

R7   T. Smith, 'Teachers and parents working together', in D. Fontana (Ed.), *The Education of the Young Child*, Basil Blackwell, Oxford, 1984.

R8   *Head Start* and similar programmes: *PAT*, Chapter 8, p. 186.

R9   I. Lazar and R. Darlington, *Lasting Effect of Early Education: A Report from the Consortium for Longitudinal Studies*, Monographs of the Society for Research and Child Development No. 195, University of Chicago Press, Chicago, Ill., 1982.

R10 J. Essen and P. Wedge, *Continuities in Childhood Disadvantage*, Heinemann Educational Books, London, 1982.

R11 G. T. Peaker, *The Plowden Children: Four Years Later*, NFER, Slough, 1971.

R12 Educational disadvantage: *PAT*, Chapter 12, pp. 272–284.

R13 Factors affecting school achievement: *PAT*, Chapter 12, p. 281.

R14 N. Radin, 'Three degrees of maternal involvement in a preschool program: impact on mothers and children', *Child Development*, **43**, 1355–1364 (1982). B. Tizard, W. N. Schofield and J. Hewison, 'Collaboration between teachers and parents in assisting children's reading', *British Journal of Educational Psychology*, **52**, 1–15 (1982).

R15 Error analysis: *PAT*, Chapter 13, pp. 309–310. See work of APU.

R16 Language skills at home and school: *PAT*, Chapter 8, pp. 170–180, 183–188. See also the references to Tough's work in the same chapter, Notes and References 33 and 34.

R17 J. Tough, 'How young children develop and use language', in D. Fontana (Ed.), *The Education of the Young Child*, Basil Blackwell, Oxford, 1984.

R18 *Schools Council's Skills in Early Childhood Project*. Materials published by Ward Lock Educational, London from 1976. Details of project from the SCDC and SEC – see end of the table in the Appendix.

R19 Gagné's work: *PAT*, Chapters 6, pp. 133–135 and 16, pp. 364–365. Piaget's work: *PAT*, Chapter 7, pp. 145–157.

R20 Concept development: *PAT*, Chapter 7, pp. 140–155 and 157–162. Language development: *PAT*, Chapter 8, pp. 170–180. Intellectual development: *PAT*, Chapter 9, pp. 194–196 and 206–212.

R21 P. H. Mussen, J. J. Conger, J. Kagan and A. Huston, *Child Development and Personality*, Harper and Row, New York, 1984. K. Sylva and I. Lunt, *Child Development: A First Course*, Basil Blackwell, Oxford, 1982. A. Branthwaite and D. Rogers, *Children Growing Up*, Open University Press, Milton Keynes, 1985.

R22 Reactions to success and failure: *PAT*, Chapters 3, pp. 48–54, 11, pp. 243–245 and 12, p. 282.

R23 L. Cohen, *Educational Research in Classrooms and Schools*, Harper and Row, London, 1976.

R24 'Need for achievement', 'fear of failure', 'levels of aspiration': *PAT*, Chapter 3, pp. 44–54.

Appendix: Examples of Projects Funded by the Schools Council

Subject	Duration	Age-range (2–19)	Project
Creative studies	1970–83	~2–11	Music Education of Young Children (*Time for Music*) T/P/AV
	1973–83	~11–18	Music in the Secondary School Curriculum T/P/R/AV
	1981–83	~14–16	Critical Studies in Art Education
	1976–82	~13–16	Art and the Built Environment T/R/AV
English	1973–83	~7–13	Communication Skills Project T/AV
	1973–77	~7–8	Extending Beginning Reading R
	1973–76	~9–13	Effective Use of Reading R
	1977–78	~11–16	Language Across the Curriculum R
	1978–81	~12–16	Reading for Learning in Secondary Schools T
	1975–79	~16–19	English 16–19 T/R/X
Humanities	1973–79	~5–11	Religious Education in Primary Schools: Development Project T/P/AV
	1971–81	~8–13	History, Geography and Social Science 8–13 (*Place, Time and Society*) T/P/AV/B
	1972–83*	~13–16	History 13–16 T/P/R/X/AV
	1970–85	~14–16	Geography for the Young School Leaver T/P/X/AV
	1976–84	~16–19	Geography 16–19 X
Inter-related studies	1979–86	~5–13	Health Education 5–13: Special Education Extension T/P
	1980–83	~8–13	World Studies 8–13 T
	1978–82	~16–19	Machine Assisted Teaching Project T/P/AV

Category	Project	Dates
Inter-related studies	Studies in the Multi-ethnic Curriculum R	1978–79
	Careers Education and Guidance (*Work*) T/P/B	1971–81
	Communications and Social Skills through Pupil use of Audio-Visual Media T/P/R	1976–82
	Industry Project T/P/R	1977–83*
	Health Education 13–18 T/P/B	1977–83
	Computers in the Curriculum T/P	1973–84
	Skills for Adult Working Life	1980–84
Languages	Cambridge School Classics Project T/P/R/X/AV	1966–80
	Teaching of Languages other than French R	1979–80
	Graded Tests in Modern Languages RX	1978–80
	Modern Languages Project T/P/X	1967–75
Mathematics	Low Attainers in Mathematics R	1978–81
	Statistical Education 11–16 (*Statistics in your World*) T/P/R/B	1975–84
	Use of Electronic Calculators in the Teaching of Mathematics at Secondary Level T/P	1978–80
	Continuing Mathematics Project T/P/R/AV	1971–81
	Mathematics and the Young Entrant to Employment R	1978–79
Organisation and resources	Evaluation and the Teacher: An Introduction to Curriculum Review and Pupil Assessment T/AV	1978–86
	Teachers' Centres – their Role and Functioning R	1979–81

Appendix (*contd.*)

Subject	Duration	Age-range	Project
Organisation and resources	1980–81		Teachers in Partnership – Four Studies of Collaboration in In-Service R
Science	1967–75		Science 5–13 T/R
	1978–84		Learning through Science T/P/B
	1978–81		Studies in Decision-making for Science Education T/R
	1969–82		Integrated Science Project (*Patterns*) T/P/X/AV
	1981–86*		Review of the Secondary Science Curriculum
	1976–83		Modular Courses in Technology T/P/X/AV
Special education	1975–79		Education of Disturbed Pupils R
SCDC† continuation funding	1981–85		The Mother Tongue Project
	1981–84		Finding Answers to Disruption
	1981–86		Guidelines for Review and Institutional Development in Schools (GRIDS)

Key

T Teacher; P Pupil material; R Report; X Tests or examinations (for pupils); AV Audio-visual material; B Broadcasting links

* Continued funding by the School Curriculum Development Committee

† The Schools Council was replaced by the School Curriculum Development Committee (SCDC) and the Secondary Examinations Council (SEC) in 1984

3

Instructional Management – Preactive Stage

There are two important stages in the process of instructional management – preactive and interactive. By preactive instructional management is meant the planning and preparation necessary prior to actually taking a lesson. This chapter and part of the last are concerned with this aspect of instruction. Chapter 4 and parts of Chapters 5 and 6 will be concerned with interactive instructional management, which is all those educational activities necessary for the progress of the lesson itself.

PREPARATION AND PLANNING

Being explicit about the purposes, methods and outcomes of lessons is a crucial part of professional development. Preparation and planning are needed to clarify one's ideas about the educational progress of a lesson, to fit the proposed lesson into a coherent scheme of work, to act as an *aide-mémoire* to improve presentation and evaluation, and to inform others (the head teacher, teachers, parents). Some schools require a regular return of overall plans (or even lesson plans), particularly from beginning teachers. Experienced teachers may often give the impression that they do not have plans or do not need to prepare lessons. Years of experience do help to implant schemes of work, but most teachers use some form of planning – even if it is done in quiet moments, in the head. Even so, making explicit the plans for lessons irrespective of experience is a necessary part of professional development.

There are broadly three levels at which planning can take place. The first and most inclusive involves the overall *syllabus* (or *course*) *objectives*. In a primary school, this may be a year's work planned by a teacher for one class; in a secondary school, it may be an introductory year in a new subject for the pupils in a class or a whole CSE or GCE course covering several years.

The second level involves *unit* (or *section*) *objectives* occurring within a syllabus, and it usually takes several lessons to complete. A topic (e.g. Roman York, tropism, percussion instruments for primary-school orchestras) might be spread over several weeks and taken intermittently or as a block of lessons in one or more consecutive weeks. The third level of planning is the lesson itself (*lesson objectives*).

Most schemes of work which students are required to prepare for teaching practice consist of the second and third levels of planning. There are several useful books which give specific guidance in scheme and lesson planning (e.g. Cohen and Manion, R1). Here, we are concerned largely with those aspects of schemes or particular lesson plans which might be informed by a knowledge of psychology.

A scheme of work, at the very least, should indicate: details of the school (location, catchment, etc.), the subject being taught, the class, details of the pupils (age, sex, ability or mixed, size, etc.). In addition, there should be information about the number and length of lessons, aims of the whole scheme, background of knowledge already possessed by pupils, content to be covered in the scheme, and special organis- ational factors (in a laboratory, gym, in the school playground), equipment needed for the scheme, and any evaluation procedures neces- sary for the overall scheme (test at the end, running profile). Cohen and Manion (R1) give helpful examples of schemes drawn up using the above criteria.

LESSON PREPARATION

Many of the issues discussed under this heading can also be applied to schemes of work. Lesson preparation is an obligatory part of all teacher- training courses. Teaching-practice files (or notebooks) are common to these preparations. As in the previous chapter, where there is further expansion of psychological ideas, cross-references to *PAT* are made.

The teaching-practice file requirements are fairly consistent and the summary below is typical of the list of demands made of students in their preparation. Indeed, part of the assessment of teaching practice is based on the soundness of the content of the file. The rest of this chapter will be devoted to an elaboration of these requirements:

(a)   clearly stated and defined objectives;
(b)   appropriateness of the objectives;

(c)   relevant and appropriate content;
(d)   student understanding of the content, concepts and skills
       needed;
(e)   suitable selection of methods;
(f)   suitable selection of materials;
(g)   clear statement of the evaluative procedures to be used;
(h)   adequate preparation of the classroom, laboratory, gym, etc.,
       before the lesson begins.

Objectives

To make a clear, unambiguous statement about the purposes of a lesson
is not an unreasonable expectation from any teacher. Without a notion
of what is to be achieved at the end of a lesson, it would be impossible to
decide on what to do in the lesson. How can one choose a route without
knowing the destination?

Theorists in the field of curriculum design like to distinguish between
aims and *objectives* (R2). In everyday language we tend to use the terms
synonymously. However, technically the term *aim* is reserved for broad
statements of the goals which are desired. They tend to appear most
frequently in the first level in planning overall syllabuses. Aims are often
value-laden (e.g. to help children appreciate the need for defence
expenditure; to inculcate tolerance to all religions). Some are so broad
they would require a whole way of life to ensure they were achieved!
Governments (and associated reports) often specify aims. Schools, as
part of a public system of education, will be influenced by these govern-
mental aims, and these broad desiderata are transmitted downwards to
local education authorities and heads of schools. Aims will not be of
concern to us here.

Objectives are much more specific statements of the behavioural
changes we hope to achieve as a result of learning experiences. One
important difference between aims and objectives is that the latter not
only specify goals, but say something about how they might be reached.
Objectives should usually state *who* is performing, *what* is required in
performance (stated by an active verb), and the conditions for
performance (P1, p. 45).

A fruitful starting point before getting involved in any details is to
decide on the emphasis of a lesson and adopt informal *planning*, before
proceeding with detailed plans. This is well covered in Barnes (R3). He
identifies five categories or focal points for lesson requirements from the
pupils, which will help to clarify the direction of the lesson. The cate-

gories are content, concepts, skills, problem-solving and interest. Table 3.1 should be informative (D1, p. 45). It is important to note that the categories rarely appear in isolation. One may be the major focus of a lesson, but the others are most likely to be involved to some degree in some lessons some of the time. It would be difficult to think of lessons which only possessed content or skills, for example.

Table 3.1   *Planning techniques used for different subjects and different teaching methods.*

	Basis	*Description*	*Subject matter*
(a)	Content	Based on an area of experience, a body of knowledge, or a group of phenomena, e.g. 'My brother's keeper', 'the Norman Conquest', 'floating and sinking'.	Most subjects, especially in their elementary stages. Can be interdisciplinary. Suited to subjects such as science, history, geography, environmental studies, religious education, literature.
(b)	Concept	Based on a concept or interrelated set of concepts; e.g. 'probability', 'energy', 'role', 'population'.	Any subject, especially in its advanced stages.
(c)	Skills	Based on a set of skills.	Some subject areas such as mathematics or literacy or craft can more readily be defined in terms of skills than in any other way. In others, such as history and art, skills play a more subordinate role.
(d)	Problem	Planning based on problems that pupils are to solve, as a means of enabling them to apply skills in a more complex and realistic situation or as a means of indirect access to concepts.	Can be used anywhere, but especially in skills-based subjects, such as mathematics, design and physical education and in some approaches to science.
(e)	Interest	Since the onus is on the learner to select issues important to him, the teacher's role is to offer a starting point and a range of possible options and methods.	Not predetermined by the teacher. Likely to be interdisciplinary and diffuse.

From D. Barnes, *Practical Curriculum Study*, pp. 5–6,   Routledge and Kegan Paul, London, 1982. Reproduced with permission.

Content-based planning

This kind of planning, based on a body of knowledge, is the commonest. As can be seen from Table 3.1, most school subjects have the potential to offer this kind of planning because they are built on a foundation of knowledge and experience. An example to be given later in the chapter, taken from Gronlund's work in planning a series of lessons on weather maps, contains several objectives which are clearly content-based. 'Write a definition of each term' (to do with weather maps), 'know map symbols' are obviously technical aspects of weather-map reading. Of course, concepts enter into this as well, because explicitly the actual weather events are being represented by a symbolic system and the concept of symbolic representation would have to be understood before progress could be made.

Concept-based planning

This is not unlike the content-based approach, except that the starting point is a concept. This approach relies very much on the disciplines which form the subjects of the curriculum. Momentum in physics, water conservation in the humanities, time or multiplication in primary teaching, counterpoint in music, leadership in history or psychology or sociology are examples of concept-based topics. It is more frequent to find concept-based lessons in the more advanced stages in teaching subjects, although arithmetic has much concept-like work in it throughout the syllabus (rules of number, decimals, fractions, etc.). Science is also particularly concept-based in the way it is taught at present.

Skill-based planning

Cognitive skills such as analysing, observing, hypothesising are common in science and mathematics. Practical skills are also self-evident in craft, physical education, music, art, drama, dance, etc. Some of the early work in infant and junior school requires skills of manipulation, such as handling materials, building, moulding, writing. Reading also necessitates a set of physical skills. Sometimes the content is incidental – a means to an end. My house is littered with objects fashioned in wood and clay – 'keepsakes' of my children's rudimentary manipulative skills at home and school. We call them 'ornaments'.

Problem-based planning

The teacher chooses a problem for the children to solve. The idea is to help the pupil in learning how to apply knowledge and thereby increase understanding. Examples from mathematics and science are plentiful. In craft, design and technology there is a decided movement toward increased use of problem-solving design exercises ('design a device for cropping apples or pears that cannot be reached easily from the ground, without having to climb too high up the fruit trees').

Interest-based planning

Sometimes a teacher might want to give children an enjoyable educational experience to stimulate interest. There is frequently a learning objective behind the experience, but the primary object is to capture the imagination and motivation of the child. Illustrations of this are field trips, films, dramatic experiences in or outside the school (e.g. inviting a group of professional artists, singers, dancers to talk to a group of children). The ideas of interest-based planning are often generated by the children – crafty teachers gain a lot from informal discussions about things which might excite the educational interests of pupils.

The act of making explicit what you hope to achieve and how this is to be done is an exacting and necessary process, but a fundamental question is how much detail is needed? Several curriculum developers in the USA (e.g. Mager, Gronlund, R4) are highly specific and very detailed, so much so that each statement could be converted into a set of questions for evaluation of the lesson (questions for the pupils). In fact, Gronlund's intention was to tabulate the objectives so that they would possess the necessary content for a criterion-referenced test (see *PAT*, R5). An example of this detailed analysis follows. It is taken from a set of classroom instruction texts designed in the USA (Gronlund, R6) and intended to illustrate criterion-referencing. It is part of a programme for teaching the science of weather. The objectives are broken down into four major areas, and within each one there are several subsidiary objectives. The four major ones are given below, with the first expanded to illustrate the amount of detail required in a behavioural analysis of objectives. The pupil should:

(a)   *know* basic terms:
      write a definition of each term;
      identify the term that represents each weather element;
      identify the term that best fits a given weather description;
      match the term to a picture of the concept;
      distinguish between correct and incorrect uses of the terms;
(b)   *know* map symbols:
(c)   *know* specific facts:
(d)   *interpret* weather maps:

Notice three points about this kind of detailed analysis. First, every possibility is covered by the objectives. Second, the teaching purpose is made quite clear in terms of the learning outcomes. Third, the verbs depicting what is to happen are unambiguous. (For further examples and a critique of behavioural objectives analysed in detail, see Barnes, R3) (D2, p. 45).

When non-behavioural objectives are included, the terminology tends to be looser, e.g. 'to further ...', 'to understand ...', 'to appreciate ...', 'to enjoy ...'. For instance, some common objectives one reads are 'to give practice in reading (or creative writing or the use of water colours)', 'to arouse interest in the study of electricity', 'to improve understanding of the use of decimals'. These examples seem at first sight to be worthy purposes. On deeper consideration, however, they give little away as to exactly how they could be achieved. How, for instance, does a teacher help pupils to improve understanding – what particular processes and what outcomes will enable and measure this? Have clear in your mind what the whole process will be in trying to achieve an objective (Cohen and Manion give some helpful comparisons of behavioural and non-behavioural statements, R1, pp. 47, 49, 51).

Whatever else, objectives should be realistic, appropriate and capable of being translated into learning experiences in the classroom. They should be written in terms which are recognisably classroom-oriented. They should also be capable of evaluation. Setting goals where you cannot judge if they have been achieved is not a sensible activity.

PRACTICE AND OBSERVATION ACTIVITIES

P1 You need as much practice as you can get in setting out objectives. On observation or early on the first teaching practice, discuss with teachers in the school (and supervisors) the objectives behind particular lessons they are teaching. Note the range, the specificity, the realistic nature of the objectives.

DISCUSSION AND ANALYSIS ACTIVITIES

D1 Read the five categories for lesson requirements in Barnes (R3, Chapter 1). In one of your teaching subjects, choose and discuss in tutorials portions of the school syllabus which could readily and appropriately be approached using the five categories – use all five one at a time.

D2 Take one of the topics from D1 above and elaborate it in some detail in the way suggested in the behavioural objectives approach. Examine the strengths and limitations of this approach.

Appropriateness of objectives

In addition to a clear statement of the objectives of a lesson, it is also necessary to take into account their relevance to the circumstances in which the student-teacher is placed (P2, p. 46). Many considerations (too many in several respects) have been mentioned in other chapters of this book which impinge on the present stage of lesson preparation. Matters such as the age of pupils, interests, needs, abilities, backgrounds, previous experience, classroom and school contexts are essential ones. Indeed, the entry characteristics discussed in the last chapter are now the focus of attention for lesson planning.

To ask a student to gather and assimilate all this kind of knowledge prior to teaching practice is a tall order. This is especially the case in secondary schools, where the number of pupils involved will probably run into the hundreds. The information will have to be obtained in stages. Some judgements are made at a general level, whereas others are very specific to, for example, particular difficulties of a child. Some of the general information can readily be obtained on preliminary visits to the school. Such things as the age, ability mix, catchment-area characteristics, *broadly* the conceptual competence of the pupils, some ideas about the previous academic experience of the pupils can be obtained on visits. But specific details of individual differences of pupils (apart from some preliminary hints from experienced teachers in the school about extreme problems – academic or behavioural), home-background influences, self-concept of ability or particular 'blind-spots' of a child will have to wait until the first lessons before they are explored sufficiently for the student to act on the information. Some forewarning of academic and behavioural problems is often helpful for defining the limits of the work to be covered, but one has to be very careful not to prejudge (self-fulfilling prophecy, R7).

Once the initial stage of the practice is over and it is a reasonable

---

PRACTICE AND OBSERVATION ACTIVITIES

P2 Ask teachers when they are going to take a class for the first time, how they gather relevant information. In the first few lessons, do they have systematic ways of gathering further information? What do they regard as the most useful *kinds* and *sources* of information? Why are they so regarded?

Take into consideration all the criteria listed in the first paragraph of this subsection on the appropriateness of objectives.

expectation that students 'know' their pupils, the teaching-practice supervisors will expect students to know sufficient about the content, concepts, skills, level of problem-solving ability appropriate to the developmental level and previous experience of each pupil in order to plan lesson objectives effectively. The appropriateness of the topic chosen, how it fits into the scheme and some knowledge of the pupils' backgrounds will be expected and looked for as part of the lesson planning.

Selection of content

In Chapter 2, we gave brief thought to the specialist subjects of study for secondary teachers and the broad general knowledge required by the primary-school teacher. Teachers responsible for the subject or class to be taken by a student on teaching practice are generally the main source of information for indicating what areas the student might tackle. Sometimes a special area is chosen for a student. Occasionally, the student is given free rein.

The content must be scrutinised from several angles. The student should be able to demonstrate through the subject matter selected and analysed that (s)he has a knowledge of the subject being taught, its structure and thence how it can be broken down into appropriate segments which will assist the pupils' learning. Also, in terms of concepts and skills (s)he will need to show how the content might be sequenced and what is a suitable portion of material for the time allowed for the lesson. All this area of activity is the province of the method tutors.

Selection of methods

Again, this part of a student's plans should have benefited from the method lecture course. The objectives, content and pupils' ability will to some extent dictate the most appropriate methods. The key to deciding on the most effective methods is by finding the best learning experiences for the material in question. The 'theories of instruction' mentioned in Chapter 6 of *PAT* have grown in response to this problem of how to fit objectives—content—methods—evaluation together. Bruner (R8) proposes that we pay attention to the most effective 'sequence' in which materials should be presented, and argues that optimal sequences need to be judged in terms of an individual's speed and power to learn, transfer possibilities, economy of learning in keeping with the 'cognitive strain' imposed and the ability of the material thus learned to help in generating new ideas.

The methods selected should demonstrate progression of learning experiences related to the overall scheme of work. There should be an appropriate balance of learning and teaching strategies – not all chalk and talk or group activity, not all private enterprise with minimal guidance. Methods should also be chosen which are appropriate to the subject area, e.g. demonstration and practical work (ideal for experimental and practical subjects), oral work (modern languages), creative interests (literature, drama, design). The lesson notes should also reflect skills in anticipating the organisational needs of children, classroom arrangement, space, resources (D3).

DISCUSSION AND ANALYSIS ACTIVITIES

D3 The questions surrounding the presentation and sequencing of content in the process of instruction is a central theme in psychology. In *PAT* Chapters 4–6 and 16, there are many references to this kind of work. Look particularly at the work of Ausubel, Bloom, Bruner and Gagné for ideas about these issues. These require careful consideration in tutorials.

Selection of materials

Instructional materials are now commonplace in education. Their appropriate use is another question. Research reported in Chapter 5 indicates that some practical sessions are used as a way of filling in time rather than as a learning event. Setting children to do practical work which does no more than keep hands busy is unacceptable. Therefore it is essential to have clearly stated in teaching-practice notebooks the precise function and usage of practical materials.

The term 'materials' covers a lot of possibilities. It is frequently and erroneously assumed that beginning students or teachers know 'instinctively' what sorts of aids will be most appropriate for their lessons. This is not so and many method lecturers spend a lot of time in elaborating this topic.

Romiszowski, in a very useful book on the selection and use of instructional media (R9), sets out a flow chart for decisions about the selection of the most appropriate media to accompany a lesson (Figure

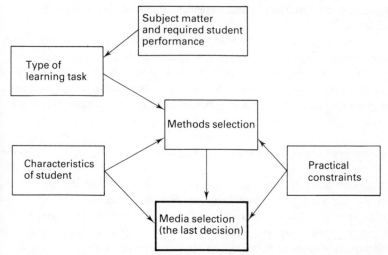

Figure 3.1 Factors influencing media selection. From A. J. Romiszowski, *The Selection and Use of Instructional Media*, p. 57, Kogan Page, London, 1974. Reproduced with permission.

3.1). The first thing to notice about the figure is that the selection of suitable media is the *last* decision to be made. This is because the final decision is contingent on a variety of other decisions. The figure shows that the content (subject matter) and pupil requirements by the teacher (assessment and/or evaluation procedure) will affect the decision. For example, the preparation of a chemical (say, copper sulphate crystals) in a science lesson is more appropriately done by either a demonstration or the pupil's practical involvement than by using a textbook description. If the learning task involves debate or discussion, there are certain kinds of media arrangements which are more appropriate. For example, a large group in a lecture theatre is not the best way of encouraging detailed small-scale discussions. Holding a book up is similarly doomed to failure in a large room. If one is teaching keyboard skills (piano or typewriter), it seems obvious that a keyboard should be present.

'Methods selection' relates to the range of possible methods of presentation (narrative presentation by teacher, individuals or groups working independently, oral or practical work by pupils, etc.). Each method has particular media which are most appropriate. This also relates to 'practical constraints', because the method proposed has to be within the resources available at the school. Not every child will have a tape-recorder or TV set. Indeed, not every child will necessarily have a textbook! The age, ability, previous knowledge of the pupils will also dictate the kinds of material which are usable. Textbooks are not much good for non-readers. Delicate apparatus will not last long with small children.

Again, this is really the province of the student's method lectures. The range of possible media and materials available is extensive. The study of audio-visual aids is a specialism in its own right, and you are recommended to read the appendices of Cohen and Manion (R1). These give a wide range of references to books and source materials (D4, p. 50).

Assessment of success in realising objectives

If you set goals for your pupils, you have to know whether they have been achieved. Chapter 6 concentrates on different methods of assessing scholastic progress and you will need to refer to that chapter (and *PAT*, Chapter 13) for some guidance about the details of assessment methods. Here it is sufficient to point out that *before* a lesson commences it is wise to know clearly how you intend to establish that learning has taken place.

Details of the tests and methods of measuring progress need to be spelt out. Testing, formal or informal, does not necessarily take place in every lesson. The learning programme may be cumulative and there may be two or three sessions before learning is tested. However, it is not wise to go too long before revision and assessment takes place.

PRACTICE AND OBSERVATION ACTIVITIES

P3 Those specialist student-teachers who will be responsible for equipment should investigate the procedures in any of the schools they visit. Also take the matter up with specialist tutors.

DISCUSSION AND ANALYSIS ACTIVITIES

D4 Figures 3.2 and 3.3 are taken from Romiszowski's book (R9) and relate to decisions for selecting visual, verbal and sound media. Inspect these figures and review as wide a range of topics as you can in terms of the selection of media. Discuss these as part of your method course. It may be possible to pool a considerable amount of material in the group. The important thing is for *you* to end up with a clear idea of *your* criteria for deciding on the most appropriate media.

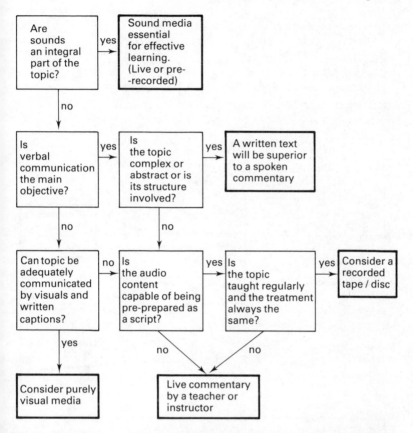

Figure 3.2 Decisions for selecting verbal and sound media. From A. J. Romiszowski, *The Selection and Use of Instructional Media*, p. 72, Kogan Page, London, 1974. Reproduced with permission.

In addition to evaluating the children's progress, it is always useful to leave a section in the notes for some personal comments about the *progress of the lesson from your viewpoint*. It sometimes happens that a lesson goes wrong and you need to make some note of the reasons why this occurred for future reference. Refer to Chapter 6 below for some further work on this section.

Organising the classroom before the lesson

Apart from the written preparation dealt with in the foregoing, there are usually a dozen and one things to do before a lesson begins in readiness

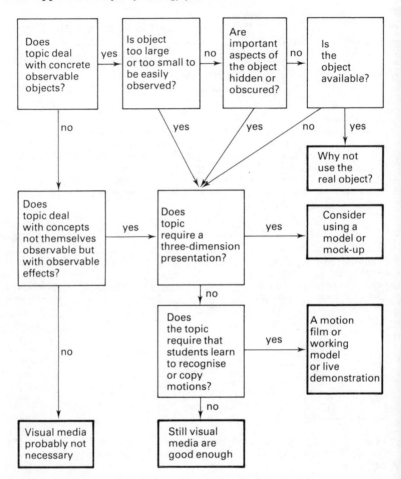

Figure 3.3 Decisions for selecting visual media. From A. J. Romiszowski, *The Selection and Use of Instructional Media*, p. 73, Kogan Page, London, 1974. Reproduced with permission.

for the lesson. In busy classrooms this might have to be done in the morning before the day's teaching begins, at lunch time or during breaks.

Classroom-based work often involves the distribution of materials, blackboard preparation, aids to be pinned up, equipment to be set up and tested (making sure the TV is plugged in and works). In laboratories, one has to make sure that the equipment is available and working. Gymnasia can be littered with equipment – often the pupils are made responsible for bringing out and returning equipment. Craft tools, equipment, materials have to be available and in working order. These subjects have routines for the care of equipment. Children also need to be taught this (P3, p. 50). Distribution of equipment, and/or its care should be noted in the teaching-practice file.

REFERENCES

R1   L. Cohen and L. Manion, *A Guide to Teaching Practice*, Methuen, London, 2nd edn, 1983.

R2   Aims and objectives: *PAT*, Chapter 16, pp. 358–368.

R3   D. Barnes, *Practical Curriculum Study*, Routledge and Kegan Paul, London, 1982, Chapter 1 especially.

R4   R. R. Mager, *Preparing Instructional Objectives*, Fearon, Belmont, California, 1962. N. E. Gronlund, *Stating Objectives for Classroom Instruction*, Macmillan, London, 1978.

R5   Criterion-referenced testing: *PAT*, Chapters 9 and 13, pp. 199–201 and 305–306.

R6   N. E. Gronlund, *Preparing Criterion-referenced Tests for Classroom Instruction*, Macmillan, New York, 1973.

R7   Self-fulfilling prophecy: *PAT*, Chapter 3, pp. 53–54.

R8   J. S. Bruner, *Toward a Theory of Instruction*, Norton, New York, 1966.

R9   A. J. Romiszowski, *The Selection and Use of Instructional Media*, Kogan Page, London, 1974.

4

The Organisation of Learning

This and the next chapter might have been written as one. Managing the physical and social conditions in a classroom is closely tied to the organisation of learning. Unfortunately, as I began to write such a chapter, it became unwieldy and the decision to split these concerns was made. Provided the two chapters are considered together or sequentially, it is hoped that their coherence is not lost.

The major concern in formal education is the quality and quantity of learning. The central activity in primary, secondary and tertiary education is the stimulation and advancement of learning, especially, but not exclusively, academic learning. Of all the social sciences, psychology has had the most to contribute in the field of theory and practice in learning, and subsequent pages will endeavour to relate this contribution to classroom work. The chapter is about some of the important findings and these are linked to theoretical underpinnings and practical ways in which they can be tried out.

As mentioned earlier, the roles of the supervisor are paramount. My grave reservations about extensive blocks of school practice have already been mentioned, and I believe that a more specific skill and task analysis approach should be used. One of these roles is to present students with as many permutations of significant aspects of classroom life as time will permit. The important point for the tutor is to provide the student with a basis from which decisions can be made – many of them rapid, on-the-spot decisions. Adaptability to particular circumstances in a lesson, each being unique, is crucial. Therefore it is not possible to provide a static blueprint for action, because the action needed will depend on the special conditions prevalent. The tutor and student can agree on destinations, or particular goals to be achieved, but the possible pathways have to be negotiated and possibly modified *en route*. That is why it is important to provide as many examples as possible, to show variety of experiences so as to expose the student to the widest repertoire from which to make decisions. There is *no one way* of solving a problem in classroom practice.

A primary difficulty in discussing classroom activity or a skill is defining the level of complexity. We tend to skip from one level of complexity to another without any clear statement. One reason for this is our lack of knowledge about skills and subskills necessary to undertake and complete various tasks in teaching. Some authors take very broad objectives (e.g. problem-solving in lessons, concept learning, motivation). Others, as in microteaching or social skills analysis, are more specific. In the following chapter, I tend to discuss broader issues and leave it to tutors to decide on the specifics and on devising ways of expanding them.

This chapter looks at five major components in the progression of a lesson and breaks these down, not as subskills, but as areas for analysis, observation and practice, with tutors alongside to draw on the subskills. The five components are *getting a lesson started, exposition, keeping the lesson going, reinforcement* and *rounding the lesson off*. Some aspects, such as seeing a class for the first time, deal with 'bricks and mortar' questions; others, such as exposition, are much deeper in both content and application.

GETTING THINGS STARTED

Experience teaches us how easy it is to get off on the wrong foot with someone else. A casual word or gesture can so easily be misunderstood. This effect can be multiplied in a class of children. The flow and 'feel' of a lesson or part of a lesson is often established at the beginning, and if matters go wrong, it is difficult to recover. Social psychologists have made some interesting studies of social interaction (R1), and they have stressed the importance of verbal and non-verbal communication in the classroom – the verbal, visual or auditory uses which begin, accompany and sometimes set a seal on a relationship. These have grown into extremely complex and problematic topics in recent years. For help about the beginning of a lesson, the research is more descriptive than instructive for the student-teacher, and we are generally forced back to anecdotal experience of others (teachers, tutors, other students).

Meeting a class for the first time

As with most new encounters, meeting a class for the very first time frequently creates appreciable tensions in both the teacher and the class.

Most experienced teachers appear to support the time-honoured method of starting 'as you mean to go on' because 'well begun is half done'. Perhaps the emphasis in starting with a new class should be a strong rather than a weak one. Whatever else, you will be acting out a role. Teaching thirty to forty young people in one place at one time is not a natural human activity. It requires some acting out. As the first impressions tend to last for some time, it would not be out of place to take on the role of a confident and competent person who is in control of the situation. Age and the kind of school play a part in the way children respond to teachers, but some children try to develop expertise in detecting and working on the 'soft spots' of teachers. The further up the educational system one goes, the more blatant is the pursuit of chinks in the armour. Establishing ground rules in class is taken up in the next chapter.

Acting is an important skill in classroom life (D1, p. 59). Some events are larger than life and our responses are correspondingly exaggerated. Anyone with an audience has to work on them in order to make them receptive. Teachers need to act out events which help to establish a good working environment, sensitive to children, but at the same time making it clear that it is not in anyone's interests to have any nonsense. Being firm, friendly and fair, but avoiding being overpowering or oppressive requires great skill and self-discipline.

Starting a lesson or new topic

This involves gaining attention and providing the framework for what is to come – *orientation* (P1, p. 59). In both primary and secondary schools, the transition from one lesson to the next involves tension and effort on the part of the teacher. In secondary schools this is made additionally difficult, because the change frequently involves a new class – they come to you or you go to them. Whichever is the case, never allow too much time to be idled away. If the pupils are coming to your room, be there first and make sure they are occupied on arrival. Stragglers are inevitable when children have to move from one classroom to another, and occupational therapy for those who arrive first is necessary. When you go to them, the problems may be greater, especially if they have been left without a teacher for a while.

When the class is assembled, a teacher must ensure that they are all attending before launching into the lesson. Casual beginnings with some children not listening can easily deteriorate into unproductive, often noisy and half-hearted effort. Capturing the interests and attention of pupils (P2 and D2, p. 59) is a skilled activity and should be quite deliberately rehearsed and practised. The process of gearing pupils up and coaxing them to learn is known as *set induction* (R2). The methods used are intended to establish the right frame of reference and mind for what will follow in the lesson, and it is about getting learners ready and 'set' to go.

Various kinds of set have been defined. For our purposes the most important are *perceptual, social, motivational, cognitive* and *educational set*. *Perceptual set* is particularly significant when meeting a class for the first time. It relates to the personal attributes which influence first impressions – dress, voice, body behaviour and so forth. Usually these first impressions are temporary and become modified as one's knowledge of others increases.

One of the first tasks of settling a class down involves *social set*. It is the opening relationship of pleasantries, smiles, gestures, etc. to set the tone. Most of the time the teacher can slip from these beginnings to the first stage of the lesson. Occasionally, gentle persuasion to gain attention fails and snappier methods are needed. For example, when pupils return from an exciting event, some time is needed for them to cool down. Whatever the methods used (hand clap, louder voice, 'I'm waiting' techniques), be careful not to get trapped into prolonged efforts to gain attention. They tend to take the edge off what is to follow and give an impression that you have not got a grip on matters. If you have to use these methods frequently, begin to wonder why and get advice.

Motivational set is clearly amongst the most important. There are many references in the literature (R3) to ways of arresting the attention of learners. The use of novel, surprising, provocative stimuli are ways of introducing topics. Starting with a knotty, but fascinating problem, an example, specimen or actual object is quite common. Uncharacteristic (but not bizarre) approaches have their place, such as commencing with mime or a rehearsed entré where one of the pupils might start the lesson. Do not overdo one method, lest the novelty wears off.

Cognitive set is a complex idea. It incorporates those aspects at the beginning of a lesson or new part of a lesson which encourage mental preparedness. For cognitive set we need to (a) provide a link with previous work (transition from the familiar to the unfamiliar), (b) gain information about previous knowledge, experience and expectations of the learners, and (c) give structure to, and an outline of, what is coming in the lesson, i.e. the advance organiser of Ausubel (R4). An advance organiser is introductory information (concepts, ideas) given to learners to increase their understanding of the lesson and to enhance their prospects of organising the new material. There are occasions, however, when it is quite possible to start with a semi-structured or guided discovery method in which pupils will be required to organise and make sense of the information available. This is possible, for instance, when a process is being explored and the content is already well established or is not important for the process. Observation sessions in science, for example, can be conducted in this way (R5). Certain topics lend themselves to guided discovery techniques (e.g. in science, social science, environmental studies), although it is important to point out that learners need careful guidance in the methods of 'discovery'. The method must be learned. Again, there are occasions when one might not want to give a preview in case the 'cat gets out of the bag'. There are times when a teacher wants to build up an argument, scenario or pose a problem with the gradual help of the learners.

Educational set is a particularly interesting concept, because it refers to the distinctions between various learning styles. The extremes, defined in the research of Siegel and Siegel (R6), are '*conceptually set* subjects [who] were adversely affected by emphasizing factual rather than conceptual acquisition; conversely, *factually-set* subjects [who] were adversely affected by emphasizing conceptual rather than factual acquisition'. Learners' reactions to subjects, parts of subjects, teaching methods, various forms of examination and general study methods will be influenced by educational set. The difference between the extremes of factually-set and conceptually-set learners is that the former are predisposed to learn factual content and the latter conceptual content. This question is raised again in discussions of learning and teaching styles.

TWO CRUCIAL SKILLS: EXPOSITION AND RELEVANCE

At the business end of classroom life there are two important survival skills. Research into those qualities which pupils like to see in a teacher shows that explaining clearly and interestingly as well as having something to say are highly favoured. Other characteristics include keeping order, having a sense of humour, being fair and friendly. Learners are quickly turned off when they do not understand explanations or teachers risk taking lessons on flimsy content. These two aspects, the medium and the message, will be important to you.

Clarity of exposition (R7)

The starting point for any attempt at explanation is the pool of

PRACTICE AND OBSERVATION ACTIVITIES

P1 + P2   Whenever you can, take note of how various people start lessons or lectures or move to a new part of the lesson or lecture. List your observations under the three headings of social, motivational and cognitive set.

Social set. Were there any pleasantries to begin with? What form did they take? How did the learners react to different kinds of opening relationships? Which appealed to you?

Motivational set. How did the teacher initially obtain attention from the class? How did the lesson begin? What was the reaction of the learners?

Cognitive set. How was the lesson put into context (if it was)? Did the teacher try to fit present knowledge into previous knowledge?

Build into your earliest teaching experiences a systematic plan of different beginnings to lessons. Experiment in order to discover ways which feel most comfortable for you and rewarding for the learners.

DISCUSSION AND ANALYSIS ACTIVITIES

D1   Most members of the acting profession undergo training of some kind. This training includes playing roles, capturing audiences, observing and using feedback from audiences, how feedback influences performance and so forth. All these are important for a teacher. Why not invite an actress or actor to talk to your group about role play and discuss how these roles might be adapted in teaching?

D2   Very early in the course, the tutor should organise a discussion session in which students bring their observations about stimulating interest and share them with the rest of the group. The wider the range of experiences shared, the greater the repertoire each student can accumulate. Stress the variations which might occur because of age, sex, ability, cultural differences.

knowledge and experience which the teacher and learners bring, and the wider fund of knowledge obtainable from the literature, samples, experiment, etc. These resolve into verbal presentation or demonstration and the use of aids of all kinds, using where possible the learners' knowledge and experience.

A number of guidelines are listed below from research into verbal style of presentation. They are guidelines, *not* rules, and will be used in the practice and observation section at the end (P3, p. 62). Their main concerns are for brevity, simplicity appropriate to the level of the learners, order, fluency and use of language (D3, p. 62).

(a) Use grammatically simple presentation and make points quite explicit.

(b) Use appropriate language understandable by the age-group being taught; define all technical terms and never try to blind youngsters with science.

(c) Do not use vague or 'padding' language.

(d) Use brevity, appeal and coverage. A learner's day is packed full of different new ideas; if every description consisted of weaving webs of words around learners, they could end up paralysed and mentally inactive.

(e) Put in the main points early on, unless it is a gradual build-up lesson.

(f) Use analogy and metaphor: analogies from familiar experience or graphic metaphors help to implant ideas.

(g) Repeat ideas, when possible in a different way or by using analogies.

(h) Keep up fluency and continuity. A hesitant style can be offputting, and darting about in the content whenever the mood takes you can be fatal if you want the pupils to remember anything.

(i) Emphasise and pause for effect.

Choosing suitable media with which to illustrate, elaborate or demonstrate the exposition is a subject which will be covered in substantial detail in 'method' courses. Here we shall content ourselves with an overview from Bruner's work (R8), which postulates three kinds of learning – *enactive, iconic* and *symbolic*. He suggests that there is a progression from *enactive* learning (by doing, acting out, manipulating objects in reality) through *iconic* learning (by using representations in models, films, photographs, illustrations) to *symbolic* learning (through the written and spoken word without needing the real thing). The progression is related to age and complexity of the task. Young children start with enactive learning (sensori-motor functioning) and gradually develop iconic and symbolic learning methods. At any age, when faced with new complex tasks or materials, most of us repeat some or all of these stages in an effort to master the tasks. Therefore careful consideration of age, task complexity and availability of media to exemplify the content of the lesson is a must.

Subject-method teaching time is given over to examining the variety and appropriateness of materials, practicals, models, films, photographs, illustrations, books and so on available in subject areas. Two immediate decisions are uppermost. One is to decide on the appropriate kind of material, given that it is available. The other is to decide when and how to utilise it (this is broached in Chapter 3, in the selection of instructional media). Timing is of the essence. As part of an attempt to retain children's interest, pay particular attention to the point at which to use illustrations (R9).

Having something to say: relevance

Children have an instinct for detecting those who, no matter how charming they may be, have nothing to say. Flannelling is doomed to failure. You need to be well organised and knowledgeable in the subjects you are teaching, keeping an eye open for commonplace examples and illustrations of your topics.

Lesson notes are an essential part of a teacher's life, as we have seen in a previous chapter. The school-practice version of lesson notes, generally much fuller and more analytical, is an important means of ensuring that the student becomes proficient in lesson preparation and evaluation. Notes serve at least three functions. First, they concentrate the mind on the content and procedures thought to be most appropriate for the lesson. Second, they enable the student or teacher to form a clear idea of the ground to be covered in the lesson, and third, they should ensure that the student has a source of reference, if it becomes necessary. If you need them, use them.

Always have some material in reserve. All teachers at some time run out of the *relevant* material they have prepared before the end of a lesson. Timing, presentation and the rate at which a class is working need practice, and you may find on some occasions that you have galloped through a lesson faster than anticipated. Be equally vigilant against spinning the content out beyond its useful limits. Revision is, of course, a recommended strategy, but it could be fatal to 'over kill'. Children get bored when they feel no progress is being made (R10).

PRACTICE AND OBSERVATION ACTIVITIES

P3 The guidelines above under the section entitled 'Clarity of exposition' contain a number of criteria which you can observe in yourself or others. Remember, you are often finding the most useful attributes for your particular approach to teaching. Work at these in order to enable you to make judgements about your own peformance.

In watching others, keep an eye and ear open for stylistically helpful procedures which you feel able to adapt for your own use.

DISCUSSION AND ANALYSIS ACTIVITIES

D3 In seminars or discussion with tutors, discuss the order of importance (if any) of the guidelines above. Other members of your tutorial group are sure to have had experiences which may cast light on the difficulties encountered in expository lessons. In method sessions, you should have ample opportunity to exploit the various media. Never look a gift horse in the mouth. Whenever useful material presents itself, collect and hoard it. Teachers with strengths in the use of visual and other aids are generally incurable hoarders.

KEEPING THE LESSON GOING

Beginning a new lesson with the novelty, change of direction, 'fresh start' which this brings will usually generate a captive class, but keeping the momentum going for the whole period requires all the resources a teacher can muster. Recent HMI surveys (R11) and research (R12) reflect a growing concern that a few teachers use the device of filling in time with unchallenging work of little educational value. To avoid this, the first necessities for maintaining the learner's concentration are stimulating, challenging, relevant material at an appropriate level in a learning environment in which the learners want to participate. In this section we shall concern ourselves with the motivational aspects and their relationship to self-concepts of achievement, methods of posing questions and reinforcement techniques.

Keeping attention

In the previous section we looked at ways of attracting attention. Interest is now turned to ways of holding the attention of learners. Stimulus variation is important at any point in the lesson (P4, p. 69). Setting tasks which are long and tedious, usually when there is little opportunity for teacher guidance in large classes, would be fatal. Ways have to be found which provide *progression* and *interaction* (with content or other people) for each individual (not an easy task in large classes) and varying sensory input.

From the teacher's viewpoint, as we said in the section on motivational set, providing novel, variable, challenging and relevant stimuli in a lively way should continue throughout the lesson (D4, p. 70). There are also presentational factors such as voice, gesture, enthusiasm, use of eyes and other non-verbal cues, movement of the teacher in the classroom, deployment of aids, grouping and regrouping of the class, all of which provide stimulus variation (R13; D5, p. 70). From the learner's point of view, there are some obvious reasons which lead to flagging attention and motivation, such as loss of interest, boring presentation, inability to cope with the level of work presented or it is too easy. Two other causes, given high motivation, are *fatigue* and *span of attention* (R14).

Judgements have to be made by the teacher as to the limit of physical and mental activity the learner can tolerate. These judgements are based on a knowledge of the learner's physical and mental development, abilities, previous knowledge and understanding. Interestingly, the conventional length of lessons in this country is a matter of history and not the outcome of research into the optimum time for exposure to a particular subject. Teachers will need to be vigilant in deciding on the most productive exposure time by watching reactions and getting feedback from children.

'Span of attention' deals with the extent of a person's ability to cope with the quantity of information presented. Do we swamp some learners by choosing too much material? The span of attention is also influenced by personality factors (R14). Extravert personalities tend not to be able to concentrate for as long as introverts. This information is only helpful as background information – awareness of possible strengths or limitations in the make-up of learners. For those who possess extreme personality profiles, the style of working has to be looked at in order to be compatible with that profile. Self-awareness of limitations or strengths is helped by teachers who are prepared to discuss (tactfully) with learners the range of possibilities. Breaks and transitions to other kinds of activities require careful management by the teacher.

The *attention needs* should be exploited to the full (i.e. curiosity, exploration and manipulation) (R15). Recent research (R12) confirms that children's interest is captured by a teacher who is prepared to use illustrations, demonstrations or experiments in an enquiring way. Play in the early years of schooling is an obvious exploitation of attention needs which teachers can utilise (R15).

There are other reasons for lack of attention and concentration which teachers should carefully monitor. A theoretical model by Maslow (R16) has some pragmatic bearing on this issue. Factors often outside the control of the teacher are present. It makes sense that children who come to school hungry, tired, unwanted at home or with little desire to achieve in school (because of lack of support from parents, for example) are less likely to fulfil the goals set at school. Teachers and the school can do much in identifying these and similar sources of difficulty and, where possible, allowing for these deprivations.

A learner's need to achieve fluctuates tremendously from time to time and topic to topic. Without a need to achieve by the pupil in those subjects prescribed in school, the teacher is presented with a tremendous task trying to find ways of rekindling the interest. The later years of secondary schooling are especially problematic – pupils frequently complain that what they are taught is not of immediate interest or relevance to them as potential post-school citizens and workers.

This low need for achievement (R17), a concept examined by McClelland (R18), is very important. Combined with it is the learner's self-concept of academic achievement and the reasons she/he attributes for her/his failure or success (R17). It seems that generally speaking those with higher need to achieve do better in school work than those who have a low need to achieve. Is it possible to encourage a learner to develop a higher need to achieve? We shall look at this question in the next section, when considering the range of factors within the competence of the teacher in deciding on strategies.

Teaching strategies and learner self-concept of achievement

A few aspects of classroom life are not controllable by the teacher, e.g. the intelligence, personality, background of the pupil, school rules, etc. Of those which are, lesson content, its presentation, teacher–learner interaction, goals and their evaluation are amongst the important aspects in contributing to keeping the lesson buoyant. Here we shall look at those aspects of teacher presentation and interaction which help to sustain the learner's participation.

Provided the work being set is within the capabilities of the pupils, it is crucial for the teacher to determine the reasons for variations in performance. Regular failure has devastating effects on a pupil. The teacher needs to lead the pupil to a point where he/she has sufficient self-knowledge to have discovered the causes of success and failure, and to be able to do something about them.

Teacher–learner interaction will include encouraging individuals to raise their level of motivation to a point where they want to succeed. McClelland (R18) recommends a number of ideas for teachers to achieve this. Some of the important ones are (a) give the learner sound, believable reasons for needing to succeed; (b) give knowledge as to how need for achievement works; (c) encourage positive attitudes to learning the motive to achieve; (d) be systematic in noting what succeeds (or fails). Research undertaken by McClelland and his associates has shown promising results, and that it is possible to create classroom environments in which the need for achievement in academic studies is raised – and correspondingly so is performance (P5 and P6, pp. 69–70).

Another factor in the realistic appraisal of self-image in achievement is the effect of success and failure on future performance and the reasons we believe to be the causes of such success or failure. The expectations and perceptions of teachers and learners of each other are believed to play some part in influencing performance (R19). Social psychologists are still not entirely confident that what a teacher expects of a learner will become self-fulfilling (R19), and the impact of this will have an effect on the learner's performance. What does seem clear is that low self-concept of academic ability is positively related to low achievement, and the teacher has a significant hand in shaping this relationship (R20).

Learners appear to attribute their success or failure to either internal or external causes, which in turn have an effect on future performance (R17). The conduct of a lesson, the reward systems associated with individuals, the verbal and non-verbal pattern which accompanies discussions about the quality and quantity of the learner's contribution, structuring a learner's activities to ensure a good measure of success (without making it a walk-over) are going to influence the reasons given by a learner for unsuccessful accomplishments. Research has not been helpful in pointing to the reasons the attributions of success or failure (e.g. abilities, effort, luck, task difficulty) come into being and in *what way* they influence performance. Teachers are thrown back onto their own observations for seeking out answers to these questions (D6, pp. 70–71).

Questioning techniques

A classroom strategy as old as the hills is that of question and answer. It is rated amongst the best and most effective ways of involving pupils at various levels of thinking. A lot has been written about the subject, especially in recent years with the increased use of microteaching, and you are recommended to consult the references (R21) for a detailed analysis. Here we shall confine the discussion to looking at when and how to ask questions and what use the teacher might make of the answers received.

Whenever the pupils' participation in exploring existing or creating new knowledge is needed, questioning is very effective. The questions may be directed to the whole class, a group or to individuals. Occasionally, spontaneous questioning may arise, but at the beginning of one's career it is wise to have most questions carefully planned beforehand. It is widely and wrongly assumed that questioning comes naturally. It does not, and the evidence seems to show that even experienced teachers spend much of their question time probing for simple recall or yes/no answers. Questions have to be worked over and subtly structured to get the best out of the pupils and the questions.

A commonly proposed division of question types is between *lower* and *higher*-level questions (Table 4.1). These reflect the level of thinking involved, if the questions are tackled adequately. Lower-level questions are those that require only the reproduction of previously learned knowledge. The method most popularly used by teachers as mentioned above – simple recall and yes/no answers – are two examples. The application of existing knowledge to arrive at *one* acceptable answer clearly obtainable from the information given (convergent thinking) is another example. Mathematical and scientific problems are often presented in this form. Higher-level questions, as the term implies, demand more cognitive effort. They require the respondents to use previous knowledge and personal judgement to analyse, synthesise and evaluate (R22) questions.

Questions must be designed to bring the best from the learners. Common usage of methods and questions requiring short recall answers does tend to instil that particular response method into children. Sometimes the cause is poor question structure; sometimes the respondents feel inhibited. How can we encourage more elaborate, relevant answers, using sounder questioning tactics? The first step is to increase learner participation in answering questions.

Redirection techniques are one way of achieving greater participation (see Perrott, R21). This is done by:

(a) constructing questions so that a single answer is not sufficient for the problem, i.e. open-ended questioning (see Table 4.1);

(b) saying as little as possible; do not over-repeat the question, but hand it round the classroom, giving clues to encourage responses ('what do you think, Jean?');

(c) making the balance of the teacher's speaking to listening in favour of the latter, even if it means nodding, pointing, first name and so on;

Table 4.1 *Order of questions.*

Order	Purpose of question	Examples
Lower order	Recall: recollection of knowledge previously learned.	(a) What is the name of the widest river running through London? (b) Can the moon be seen in the daytime – yes or no?
	Comprehension: using knowledge to show understanding without relating it to other ideas	(a) Give two differences between an insect and a spider. (b) Describe the main characteristics of a pencil.
	Application: using knowledge to solve a problem with *one* solution	(a) If $7 - 2x = 6$, what is x? (b) If force = mass × acceleration of a body, what happens to the force when a body is thrown upwards.
Higher order	Analysis: 'why' type questions, deducing causes from evidence	(a) Explain why birds' beaks seem appropriate to their eating habits. Give examples. (b) What is the evidence for believing that cream is lighter than milk?
	Synthesis: combining ideas in original ways to give several equally acceptable answers	(a) What actions could a teacher take to control an unruly pupil? (b) What would life be like if everyone woke up tomorrow with the left hand only?
	Evaluation: making value judgements and opinions	(a) Is there a place for psychology as a subject in sixth form 'A' levels? (b) The teachings of Christianity were necessary for the development of our society whether there had been a Christian religion or not. Discuss.

Based on B. S. Bloom et al, *Taxonomy of Educational Objectives. Handbook I: Cognitive Domain*, Longman, London, 1956.

(d)   encouraging pupils to respond to each other ('what do you think of Tony's answer, Louise?').

The important part about asking questions is to know beforehand what length, quality, kind of thinking you want to be generated in the children by the answers – i.e. framing questions.

Other useful devices for encouraging individuals to answer include clear wording, well-timed pauses, prompting, using 'half-open' questions or partial answers as the starting point for a more elaborate answer, and capitalising on a special interest of the pupils.

Good questions like good explanations should, according to Brown (R21), be like a bikini – brief, appealing, yet covering the essential features. Clear and unambiguous wording is essential. Also remember that questions are directed at *someone* about *something*. Subject areas have sometimes specific kinds of questions not found elsewhere. As part of the method courses it is important to discuss these variations, rather than decontextualising the questioning.

Pauses after asking a question should be the rule rather than the exception. The 'rapid-fire' question is occasionally used, but generally time is needed for learners to reflect on and compile sensible answers. The teacher needs time to watch for responses from the class and judge who might be asked. Pausing also implies that you are expecting careful thought. Also keep a mental record of the answer patterns in class. It is normally the same handful who answer. If necessary, field out the questions so that everyone at some time gets a chance. Questions should also be answered by *one* person, not several. Keep a watchful eye and ear open for those who shout the answers before you have had a chance to select someone. You do not want the noise and you do want to question in a systematic way.

Prompting is a very skilled activity. It consists of helping a respondent on to further awareness without giving too much away. It also avoids too much teacher talk, if you can wring the answers from the learners. Prompting and probing also enable the teacher on occasion to use a half answer as a starting point for further questioning or in a few cases for starting a new area.

The responsiveness of a class is likely to affect the questioning tactics of the teacher (R23). Less responsive classes need encouragement, and it is possible that teachers' questions will become more closed in order to get the class moving. A half-open question is one which encourages a yes/no answer, but also enables the respondent to go on to elaborate or justify that answer. This combination also enables the pupil to give both lower and higher-order answers (P7).

PRACTICE AND OBSERVATION ACTIVITIES

P4 Stimulus variation is vitally important in classroom activity. The following list of activities indicates ways in which a teacher can use tactics to bring about stimulus variation. For each activity, draw up an observation schedule of an experienced teacher, noting which tactics are used and making some assessment of their effectiveness.

    (a) Movement of teacher in the classroom:
        (i)   around the class;
        (ii) when speaking to the class;
        (iii) gestures (lively, still, etc.);
        (iv) eye contact;
        (v) any other movements which hinder or help the progress of the lesson.

    (b) Voice – speech pattern:
        (i)   variation, and when this happens;
        (ii) response to different kinds of pupil behaviour;
        (iii) how language is used to attract attention (focusing behaviour).

    (c) Using alternative sensory channels:
        (i)   use of visual aids;
        (ii) looking, listening, speaking, reading on the part of pupil;
        (iii) other kinds of aids – demonstration, model making, manipulating objects, etc.

    (d) Teacher–learner interaction:
        (i)   class grouping;
        (ii) how much teacher–group interaction (see work by Galton and Simon, R12);
        (iii) how much teacher–pupil interaction;
        (iv) how much pupil–pupil interaction – and what kinds of interaction are helpful.

P5 The suggestions made by McClelland (R18) and reproduced in the section headed 'Teaching strategies and learner self-concept of achievement' are well worth exploration during your observation. They are intended to raise motivational levels and:

    (a) give the learner sound, believable reasons for needing to succeed;
    (b) give knowledge as to how need for achievement works;

    (c)   encourage positive attitudes to learning the motive to achieve;

    (d)   be systematic in noting what succeeds (or fails). Examine the variety of ways by which teachers try to attain these goals.

P6   There is a very useful table of non-verbal responses helpful in teaching in Brown (R21, pp. 95–96). Students can practise these with other students or tutors. In micro-lessons or on school observation, note the wide variety of non-verbal cues passing between teacher and taught. Where possible, evaluate their effectiveness.

P7   Questioning techniques require practice. In those institutions with microteaching facilities, there will doubtless be a course on this topic. Table 4.1 showing the two levels of questioning – lower and upper order – could form the basis for several microteaching sessions of 10 minutes. Set up several short sessions in order to practise the six kinds of questions in Table 4.1. Concentrate on those methods that enable redirection techniques to be rehearsed. The quick-fire, factual type of question is comparatively easy. Go for the open-ended method in practice sessions and practise the art of prompting. In preparing for school practice, pay particular attention to the questions you propose to ask and go over in your mind the kind of thinking you are trying to encourage in the pupils by the questions you are setting.

DISCUSSION AND ANALYSIS ACTIVITIES

D4   The useful debate surrounding 'span of attention', attention needs, sensory deprivation has practical implications. The area should constitute a productive discussion in tutorials, especially after reading up the literature. Start with *PAT*, Chapter 4, pp. 77–78, the section entitled 'Perception and the teacher', and related references.

D5   Another key aspect of the problem of attention is one relating to perception. With the help of tutors, examine (possibly some simple experiments as well) the suggestion that intensity, novelty, variability, distributed regularity, colour and conditioned stimuli are variables in arresting attention. Relate these to classroom activities.

D6   Colin Rogers' book, *A Social Psychology of Schooling* (R19), puts across a number of issues raised in this section, partic-

ularly those relating to teacher and pupil expectations, self-
concept and self-esteem, attribution of success and failure. It
gives a reasoned argument for and against the generalisations
arising from the research in this area. With the tutor, read and
examine the relevant parts of this book with an eye on those
points which can be of immediate value in classrooms. Are
there differences arising from age, sex, or ability?

REINFORCEMENT

The question of the importance of reinforcement in the reward and
punishment system that can be operated in classrooms will be taken up in
the next chapter, when considering the place of applied behavioural
approaches to class management. For the present, we shall look
specifically at those positive reinforcers most commonly used by teachers
in encouraging cognitive activity. The next chapter will be more concerned with social behaviour in the classroom.

Positive reinforcement (R24) is used most regularly in praising
children's responses, either oral or written (P8, p. 72). The reward
mechanisms used to produce reinforcement can be summarised as verbal
('well done!', 'good work'), non-verbal (nods, smiles, pat on back,
facial and body gestures), token (marks, stars, points) and back-up (so
many tokens, stars, points can be used for a more substantial reward,
such as feeding the animals in the classroom, or receiving some extra
privilege).

To increase a teacher's range of reinforcers one has to look for those
aspects of classroom life that children find rewarding, many of which are
the rewards in life itself, no matter where a person is, but some are
specific to classroom life. Whatever else, the rewards must have
meaning, otherwise they will not survive. There are many to choose
from, and a little thought should produce quite a formidable list ranging
from intrinsic rewards which are difficult to objectivise (feelings of satisfaction, joy) to extrinsic rewards (the verbal, non-verbal, token rewards
mentioned in the last paragraph). Of these, we can only make guesses
about the intrinsic ones from what children say. Extrinsic factors are
observable and, to the advantage of the teacher, manipulable (P9, p.
72).

The ground rules enunciated by Skinner and his associates (R25) need
to be borne in mind when applying reward systems (D7, p. 72).

These are:

1. Make sure the learner knows exactly why he/she is being rewarded.
2. Reward should quickly follow the required behaviour (correct answer to oral question, good essay).
3. There should be consistency in the reward system. Irregular, patchy uneven systems which the children cannot fathom are obviously not going to be recognised and utilised by them.
4. Frequent reward should be applied in the early stages (continuous reinforcement) and gradually reduced as circumstances permit (intermittent reinforcement), but it is unwise to overdo the frequency of rewards if it is not necessary (learners become immune), and do not give rewards which are disproportionate to the deed – let the reward fit the deed in form and magnitude.
5. Situations should be created to enable all those in the class to be rewarded appropriately at some time.

PRACTICE AND OBSERVATION ACTIVITIES

P8   In *PAT*, Chapter 3, we talk about a 'continuum of feedback mechanisms' running from high praise to severe punishment. Explore this continuum of rewards and punishments using knowledge of school days, school observation and parental control. Which do you think are effective at particular ages, and why? Discuss the issues with children when the opportunity presents itself.

P9   Note the use which teachers make of incentives. Compare the relative merits of incentives in particular age-groups and, where possible, with different ability ranges.

DISCUSSION AND ANALYSIS ACTIVITIES

D7   What do children find rewarding in classroom life?
  (a) What influences self-concept and self-esteem?
  (b) Look at verbal responses from the teacher which might be rewarding.
  (c) Look at non-verbal responses.
  (d) What token systems are possible in primary and/or secondary schools?
  (e) What effect does age or ability have?

CLOSURE

'Closure' (Brown, R7) is a technical term for rounding off a section or a whole lesson. A ragged or half-finished ending to a lesson can be unproductive in terms of retention of lesson content and ends the teacher–pupil contact in a tense rather than relaxed fashion. These aspects of content completion and personal relationships are sometimes referred to as *cognitive* and *social closure* (P10).

PRACTICE AND OBSERVATION ACTIVITIES

P10 Note the different ways in which those you observe complete their lessons. Draw up a list of ways to round off lessons, discuss these in tutorials and experiment with them either on practices and/or microteaching.

Cognitive closure can be achieved in a variety of ways. Frequently a short written or oral test is used just to remind children of the main points. The teacher may present a summary on the blackboard or on a visual aid. Sometimes the closure is delayed for homework – 'finish this work off in your free time'. Always give pupils an opportunity to ask any final questions. It should be common practice to hear teachers ask their children at the end of a section or lesson: 'Is there anything you did not follow? Have you any questions?'

The reasons for cognitive closure are that it (a) directs attention to the need for consolidating what has transpired in the section or lesson; (b) gives the section or lesson a coherence so that pupils can identify a relevant 'chunk' of information; (c) offers an opportunity for revision of the main points; (d) enables the teacher to appraise and reinforce work well done.

Social closure, as the term implies, involves the usual pleasantries of parting. Students should not need any advice on the many ways of saying goodbye! The intention is to end the lesson on a pleasant note. There is nothing worse for either teacher or children to part at the end of a lesson on a sour note. Last impressions have a habit of sticking in the mind.

Lesson notes should always contain a statement of how it is intended to close a section or lesson. Sufficient time should always be left for this to happen. Timing is an essential, but difficult, skill in lessons and needs to be practised.

74 *Applications of Psychology for the Teacher*

REFERENCES

R1   Verbal and non-verbal communication is a topic of interest to social psychologists. L. Cohen and L. Manion, *Perspectives in Classrooms and Schools*, Holt, Rinehart and Winston, Eastbourne, 1981, Chapter 6.

R2   Set induction: *PAT*, Chapter 4, pp. 68–71, 77–78. O. Hargie, C. Saunders and D. Dickson, *Social Skills in Interpersonal Communication*, Croom Helm, London, 1981. *PAT*, Chapter 5, p. 93.

R3   Gaining attention: *PAT*, Chapter 4, pp. 68–71.

R4   Advance organisers: *PAT*, Chapter 5, pp. 110–111. B. Joyce and M. M. Weil, *Models of Teaching*, Prentice-Hall, Englewood Ciffs, New Jersey, 2nd edn, 1980.

R5   Assessment of Performance Unit (APU) findings in the teachers' occasional publications, see Chapter 6.

R6   L. Siegel and L. C. Siegel, 'Educational set: a determinant of acquisition', *Journal of Educational Psychology*, **56**, 1–12 (1965).

R7   Exposition: O. Hargie, C. Saunders and D. Dickson, *Social Skills in Interpersonal Communication*, Croom Helm, London, 1981, Chapter 7. G. Brown (1975) *Microteaching*, Methuen, London, 1975, pp. 98–99.

R8   Suitable media for Bruner's enactive, iconic and symbolic modes of learning, see *PAT*, Chapter 8, pp. 178–180.

R9   Perception: *PAT*, Chapter 4, pp. 73–78. A. J. Romiszowski, *The Selection of Instructional Media*, Kogan Page, London, 1974.

R10 Revision: *PAT*, Chapter 6, pp. 125–133.

R11 Department of Education and Science, *Primary Education in England: A Survey by HM Inspectors of Schools*, HMSO, London, 1978. Department of Education and Science, *Aspects of Secondary Education in England: A Survey by HM Inspectors of Schools*, HMSO, London, 1979.

R12 P. E. Willis, *Learning to Labour: How Working Class Kids Get Working Class Jobs*, Saxon House, Westmead, 1977. M. Galton and B. Simon (Eds), *Progress and Performance in the Primary Classroom*, Routledge and Kegan Paul, London, 1980.

R13 Sensory deprivation: *PAT*, Chapter 4, pp. 69–70.

R14 Span of attention: *PAT*, Chapters 4, p. 70, and 6, pp. 126–127 and Chapter 11, p. 268.

R15 Attention needs and play: *PAT*, Chapter 3, pp. 46–48.

R16 Maslow's hierarchy of basic human needs: *PAT*, Chapter 3, pp. 41–44.

R17 Need for achievement: *PAT*, Chapter 3, pp. 48–52. Attribution of success and failure: *PAT*, Chapter 3, pp. 52–54.

R18 D. C. McClelland, 'Towards a theory of motivation acquisition?', *American Psychologist*, **20**, 321–333 (1965).

R19 Self-fulfilling prophecy: C. Rogers, *A Social Psychology of Schooling*, Routledge and Kegan Paul, London, 1982. *PAT*, Chapter 3, pp. 53–54.

R20 Self-concept of academic ability: Rogers' reference in R19 and *PAT*, Chapter 3, pp. 53–54.

R21 Questioning: G. Brown, *Microteaching*, Methuen, London, 1975, pp. 103–118. E. Perrott, *Effective Teaching*, Longman, London, 1982, pp. 41–91. C. Kissock and P. Iyortsuun, *A Guide to Questioning*, Macmillan, London, 1982.

R22 Bloom's taxonomy: *PAT*, Chapter 16, p. 362.

R23 Problems of encouraging answers from pupils: D. H. Hargreaves, 'Teachers' questions: open, closed and half-open', *Educational Research*, **26**, 46–51 (1984).

R24 Positive reinforcement: K. Wheldall and F. Merrett (1984) *Positive Teaching: The Behavioural Approach*, Allen and Unwin, London, 1984. *PAT*, Chapter 5, pp. 98–103.

R25 Promoting reinforcement: *PAT*, Chapter 5, pp. 98–101. Also refer to Wheldall and Merrett in R24 above.

5

Classroom Management

Two kinds of educational management have been defined in the literature. They are *instructional* and *classroom management*. Instructional management was referred to in Chapter 3. In this chapter we shall concentrate on classroom management. There is some artificiality in separating out classroom management from the organisation of learning, but for convenience of presentation it is easier. The variety of issues falling within this heading are the decision-making process, management strategies, leadership, discipline, teacher styles, teacher expectations and advice to parents on study. The last topic deals with the management of study at home.

DECISION-MAKING IN THE CLASSROOM

Any kind of managing or organising requires decision-making. Yet in teacher-training we do not pay too much attention to looking at the role of decision-making in the classroom. A recent book by Calderhead (R1) shows quite convincingly the place of decision-making in the classroom and distinguishes three kinds of decisions – reflective, immediate and routine. In Chapter 3 we referred to instructional preparation, the selection of methods and content, indeed, all the 'preactive' decisions which occur prior to the actual lesson. These are examples of reflective decisions. Immediate decisions about expected and unexpected events fill out the teacher's day. The discussions in this chapter relate to the 'interactive' decisions about discipline, interrelationships and moment-by-moment deployment of material resources. Routine decisions, the automatic classroom practices, are also an essential part of the coping behaviour of teachers. Each of us has a range of routines which we negotiate with learners. Such understandings about noise levels, hands up for questions, seating arrangements and so forth are possible routines.

The student or beginning teacher presented with many dilemmas and difficulties is constantly making decisions. In order to assist in this process, one needs to consider the demands of teaching and the options open for a solution. Routine decisions are less in evidence. It takes time and experience to build up a repertoire of well-tried decisions.

Calderhead (R1) found that, on comparing experienced teachers' reactions to critical events in the classroom, a marked difference existed as a result of their 'working knowledge and demonstrates how experienced teachers have come to structure their knowledge of pupils, situations and classroom contexts together with their repertoire of teaching practices to enable classroom events to be readily identified and dealt with quickly and routinely' (P1 and D1).

PRACTICE AND OBSERVATION ACTIVITIES

P1　Reference is made to a book by Calderhead (R1). At the end of his Chapters 1 and 2, there are several exercises worth attempting. Two are particularly appropriate here. List the routines you employ for specific aspects of a lesson, e.g. starting, questioning, ending, discipline, practicals, movement, marking work, etc. Compare these routines with an observed teacher. How do you judge the relative merits of different routines?

DISCUSSION AND ANALYSIS ACTIVITIES

D1　Carry out an analysis of the characteristics of effective and ineffective classroom managers. This could be done by the tutorial group, individually to begin with and then pool the results. What special circumstances lead to different management styles? Do such factors as mixed ability, age, subject, time of day make a difference?

MANAGEMENT STRATEGIES

The last twenty years have seen a steady increase in the amount of descriptive research looking specifically at successful classroom organisation and management methods (P2 and D2, p. 80). The texts available on this topic range from chatty advice on discipline (R2), broader 'class-spun' books (R3) to books including research findings (Gnagey, R4; Wragg, R5; Calderhead, R1). Their comments, findings and experiential advice tend to be consistent.

One of the earliest and most influential pieces of research was undertaken by Kounin and associates (R6), who used classroom observation techniques including videotapes (for some detail see *PAT*, Chapter 11). Kounin observed teachers' group-management techniques, choosing extremes of successful and unsuccessful managers in an effort to tease out those qualities which distinguished them. Intriguingly, Kounin did not manage to isolate a single *consistent* variable that characterised successful or unsuccessful teachers although they all dealt with behaviour problems in very much the same fashion. Detailed study of the tapes, however, did reveal some useful positive points worthy of note which are associated with reasonable well-controlled classes.

Anticipation

Anticipation of possible sources of trouble is an asset. 'Prevention is better than cure' works especially well and seems to be the order of the day with successful teachers. The teachers who can 'suss out' a possible centre of deviant behaviour and nip it in the bud before it escalates has a better chance of surviving than one who allows matters to reach a point where disciplinary action has to be taken.

'Withitness'

This ability to spot sources of trouble Kounin called 'withitness'. It is the teacher with eyes at the back of the head, omnipresent (who always seems to be on the spot and does not miss a trick), one who has the whole class in the sights by effective scanning. It is almost tantamount to a sixth sense about the origins of children's disruptive tactics. The secrets seem to be *timing, targeting* and *temperate reaction*. One has to judge the right moment to intrude in the appearance of misbehaviour; some jump in too soon and have a repeat performance on their hands a little later. To aim at the wrong target can be disastrous. Miscreants get great pleasure from seeing others blamed for their transgressions, and the innocent, quite rightly, find it very hard to forgive the injustices of being falsely accused and condemned. Temperate reaction is needed, not over-reaction. Over-reaction can be fatal. Judging the level of reaction to particular situations is most important. Avoid overdoing the reaction to the point of loud, hysterical shouting. Move in long before this point. Tantrums from a teacher are not exactly the model one wishes to convey to pupils. The failing student is often the one who is swamped by the situation. He or she tends to concentrate on the detail of a child's problems and loses sight of the rest of the class.

Smoothness

Smoothness in keeping children at work is important. Avoid: (a) intruding when there is useful, business-like activity; (b) starting a new activity abruptly before the present one has been finished; and (c) chopping and changing activities by starting and finishing abruptly (Kounin refers to this as 'flip-flops').

Do not stay on a topic too long

Do not remain on a topic too long and avoid organisational arrangements which will slow the majority down to a pace below their competence. Flow and continuity – keeping children busy with what they see as interesting material – is effective ('they don't have time to misbehave').

Overlapping

Overlapping, or the ability to do more than one thing at once, is a useful strategy. The idea is that no child should feel able to go unobserved or unnoticed for any length of time. While helping one child, it should be possible to cast eyes around the class for disruptive behaviour.

One aspect of Kounin's work which is useful to know is that a correlation exists between successful instructional management and behavioural classroom management. In plain terms, those who have their material well prepared, who organise and present activities in tight, interesting ways tend to have fewer behavioural problems.

Another key to success found by Kounin (and confirmed in much recent research, including research by Wragg (R5, 1984)) is the extent of *teacher and pupil* involvement in lessons. There is a significant relationship between high involvement and low deviancy (the more the pupils are involved, the less time they have to be disruptive).

There are age-related differences in the above strategies. The socialisation process for the little ones forms a major part of a reception teacher's day – innocent high spirits sometimes appear. In primary school, vigilance is not such a severe problem as in the secondary age-range of 12–15 years. A host of factors – changing motivation patterns, puberty, change of teaching system, striking out for independence, teachers are not in contact for as long as in the primary school, and so on – give rise to changing attitudes and interactions between teachers and pupils. The observations of Kounin are particularly relevant to this latter age-group.

PRACTICE AND OBSERVATION ACTIVITIES

P2 Management strategies are very important. Note the successful strategies described by Kounin – anticipation, 'withitness', smoothness, not staying on a topic too long, overlapping. Observe the effect of these characteristics on practice and analyse your own approaches to the strategies.

DISCUSSION AND ANALYSIS ACTIVITIES

D2 It is very important to compare notes on the observation in P2 above. A group discussion should be arranged. It is sometimes possible to obtain videotapes of lessons, which (possibly inadvertently) demonstrate the strategies. Look at these. Also in your discussions take account of different class arrangements – grouping of pupils, narrative, class discussion, practical work, etc. Mixed ability groups may also present particular problems when applying these strategies.

LEADERSHIP AND EXERCISING CONTROL

One fundamental unit in the classroom is the group, and groups have leaders. Leaders are created for many reasons, but in the classroom the teacher must take responsibility and assume that role. The debate about appropriate leadership styles continues, although not much research has been done since the pioneer work of Lippitt and White (R7 and *PAT*). They defined three categories of leader – the authoritarian, *laissez-faire* and democratic. Authoritarians hand out orders and do not expect any questions about their authority; *laissez-faire* methods are really leaderless, and children are given a free hand in decision-making; democratic systems develop group relationships and involve the group in decision-making.

The effectiveness of these styles of leadership was judged using two criteria of productivity and enjoyment of the activity as a group (e.g. enjoyment of the relationships). Authoritarian-led groups produced more in less time. The price paid was that relationships were not good. *Laissez-faire* group leadership tended to lead to both poor production and poor interpersonal relationships. Democratically-led groups certainly develop good relationships and their production levels were nearly as good as those of the authoritarian group.

The results might suggest that democratic leadership is best. Looking at these leadership styles and thinking of the many circumstances a teacher is faced with in the classroom, it seems to me there is a place for applying all three kinds of leadership methods, judiciously and carefully planned. It would not be difficult to think of occasions when it is appropriate to show authority. Marland (R3) states that responsibility for a group means one has to be a leader – 'you have to be able to dominate the group. Obviously this is an ability that has to be used tactfully and sensitively – but it must be possible.' There are times when latitude is appropriate, say in a brainstorming session (*PAT*, Chapter 10, pp. 233–234), or in design sessions where tight or even democratic guidance might defeat the purpose of the exercise. This is an example of how achievement might be affected by leadership patterns.

Classrooms are also systems of groups, not a single group. Children associate with each other in a variety of ways forming recognisable groupings. The groups are voluntary and as such they constitute a set of people held together, because the group provides satisfaction for each of its members. These points raise a number of questions about group management which the student needs to consider. Which are the groups? Why do they cohere? What motivational need is being met from membership of the group? Who are the leaders? Why are they the leaders? How can this knowledge be used to greatest effect in, for instance, planning class activities? To what extent are the needs for affiliation, achievement, gregariousness (*PAT*, Chapter 3, pp. 41–44) being met by group membership?

How do teachers attempt to achieve the leader role? A variety of techniques have been noted by Woods (R8) in a descriptive study of secondary-school pupils. It is instructive to look at the important and useful techniques he describes (see R8, *PAT*, Chapter 11 for details of the research). These are 'socialisation', 'occupational therapy', 'domination', 'negotiation', 'fraternisation' and 'ritual and routine' (P3, p. 83). Most of these methods are used by most teachers, in moderation, and can be employed to good effect, provided they are not carried to extremes. Woods' descriptions are exemplified by extreme cases, but modest and caring use are effective.

The process of *socialisation* at home and school is essential. There are rules to every well-organised system, and living in harmony with others in a culture similarly must have its do's and don'ts. School as a mini-society is an obvious place for teaching those rules. Some rules are clearly stated, such as the laws of the land or matters of common courtesy and decency. Schools develop guidelines such as knowing about the school, classroom conduct and what some describe as the puritan or protestant ethic of 'hard work, sober living and good manners'. (Actually, if one condoned the opposite of these – laziness, intemperance and bad manners – life would be intolerable for teachers.) Students and beginning teachers need to familiarise themselves with the school traditions and help to apply them. Classroom codes are partly laid down by the school, but are mainly left to the teacher. Have a clear idea of your codes of practice, your expectations of pupils' behaviour, and strive to ensure they are followed by the class.

The term *occupational therapy* is used by Woods as a somewhat derisory way of describing the use of practical sessions as a means of killing time with dulling, but acceptable (to the pupils), activities – more in the nature of play than work. Practical work in science, housecraft, wood or metal work, drawing maps, patterns and so forth are patently part of the essentials of these practical subjects. Students must guard against the use of practical sessions as a means of occupying the class. There must be an expectation of useful outcomes. This also applies to 'duties' handed out to pupils. This is a very acceptable process of involving children in the life of the classroom. The important distinction between occupational therapy as a playway and as a practical learning device is *educational purposefulness*. There has to be a clear, but defined learning outcome, where children can still enjoy the practical work.

Domination, if it means crude physical punishments (for example, lifting children by their ears or sideburns, rapping knuckles with a block of wood or verbal abuse aimed at humiliating a child), is a totally unacceptable way of exercising authority. Domination, if it means forceful exercising of authority done compassionately, is inevitable. Later we shall take up the question of discipline in the classroom, but, for the moment, this extract from a practising head teacher which we started to quote above summarises a sensible middle road:

You have to be able to dominate the group. Obviously this is an ability that has to be used tactfully and sensitively – but it must be possible. It is pointless to be afraid of 'dominating' the pupils, whether for the sake of creating good relationships or from a wish to allow individualists to flourish.

There is amongst many young teachers a diffidence that makes them pull back from imposing their will: the result, too often, is that a clique of pupils in the class imposes its will instead. This is resented by other pupils, and the resentment sours those pupils' relationship with the teacher. Diffidence is a virtue in many circumstances, but it is dangerous in the classroom: it often allows those who are not diffident – and there are likely to be a few in every group – to dominate. [Marland, R3, pp. 9–10]

Related to the domination issue is the place of *negotiation* in applying codes of practice. About some issues in the classroom (e.g. discourtesy, excessive noise, violence, crudeness), there can be no compromise. They should not be allowed to persist. Other issues can be negotiated. Agreements about classroom behaviour are frequently mapped out by discussion between teacher and pupils. Indeed, pupils who move from teacher to teacher, as in the secondary school, experience almost as many regimes as teachers, each one having worked out a set of ground rules.

Fraternisation, or 'if you can't beat them, join them', if used sensibly, can help to bridge the generation gap by skilful identification of common interests. For example, sport (particularly football and less so cricket, tennis, hockey), physical fitness, hobbies, music ('pop' or otherwise), literature, TV are sources of common interest. What the student or beginning teacher must avoid is adopting the role of an adolescent – or even worse a young child. An embarrassing situation can easily be provoked in schools by a middle-aged 'trendy' attempting to emulate an adolescent in word and deed. Respect should be earned through having something worth looking up to, not by lowering one's sights in order to gain favour.

The human race survives by *ritual* and *routine*. Random and constant change would be both exhausting and destructive in the end. We saw earlier that life in the classroom for a teacher becomes tolerable when

---

PRACTICE AND OBSERVATION ACTIVITIES

P3 Look for examples of socialisation, occupational therapy, domination, negotiation, fraternisation, ritual and routine in classes which you watch or take. Read Woods' book (R8) and see if the other 'survival strategies' he describes are in evidence.

some decision-making, probably most of it, is routine. In fact, Woods showed that routine systems of regulated activity tended to give fewer management problems than self-paced activities.

All these devices for survival are described by Woods (R8), generally in

Table 5.1   *Ready reference chart for some common disciplinary problems.*

Incident	Possible cause	Suggested action
Your class engages in chatter and uninvited comments or asides.	Release from previous hard line teacher. Pupils not impressed by you or your lesson.	More discussion, activity. Examine your own attitude and lesson selection and preparation.
Difficult pupil; won't co-operate, becomes aggressive or insolent.	Probably a combination of home, school, social conditions, experience.	Get to know him. Infiltrate, don't victimise. Liaise with other staff.
Pupils seem bored.	School regime? Narrow (exam?) curriculum. Your lessons are dull and pointless.	Not a lot you can do about regime, but you can revise lessons and teaching methods.
High incidence of truancy and lateness.	Local area, school has general problems, not just you. Or, you seem to be a soft touch.	As far as you can, tighten up all round, get absence notes, cover yourself *always*.
Aggressive behaviour directed at you and at other pupils.	Poor home, tough area, resentment against you, the school and the world as a whole.	Get background data, but rarely are *all* pupils violent. Check causes, avoid confrontations.
Smoking, drinking, glue-sniffing.	Peer-group pressures, seeking mature status or 'kicks'. Sheer defiance of teachers.	Clamp down. Inform, yet again, about health risks. Watch teeth, fingers, eyes. *Enlist aid* of head and social workers, etc.
A pupil continually interrupts.	Attention-seeking. Bored. Hostility directed at you or your subjects.	Timetable short talk by pupil. Tell him rest of class are interested. See him later, discuss.
Cheeky and 'silly' behaviour, giggling.	Insecure. Seeks attention, or is genuine extravert.	Find out why. Enlist in oral situations: drama, discussion, debate.
Thieving.	Home background or peer group norms. Needs money for specific reason. Seeks affection.	*Liaise with other staff.* See other pupils. Drugs? Girlfriend? Find out if you can. Give such affection.
Indolent.	Poor reader. Clever, but bone idle with it. Home problem.	Deal sympathetically. Find out what he *will* do, if anything. Enlist aid through school organisation.

From R. Farley, *Your Discipline in School*, pp. 31–32, New Education Press, London, 1984. Reproduced with permission.

exaggerated circumstances. There is, however, real value in subtle and thoughtful appreciation by teachers of all the above tactics. All are aimed at establishing the teacher as leader in the exercise of control.

DISCIPLINE

For the student or new teacher, as we mentioned above, *learning how to prevent disruptive behaviour* involves a number of important skills. Controlling pupil behaviour depends to a large extent on the careful planning which has preceded a lesson and the extent to which pupils can be kept busy with interesting and relevant activities, including listening. The stress of classroom disorder is very exhausting and draining. For those students or teachers who have constant running battles consisting of such ammunition as 'quiet 4B', 'silence', 'I'm not going to tell you again' fired at regular intervals, there is something wrong. Ideally, a high level of pupil involvement through carefully laid plans of activities, the use of guidelines or norms of classroom behaviour negotiated on first meetings with a class, and an array of class management ideas mentioned above should yield a reasonable working atmosphere. But we live in a real world in which the best-laid plans sometimes come unstuck. Some pupils, despite careful planning, set out to cause trouble, and evasive action has to be taken. Mercifully, research seems to show that gross misbehaviour is very rare. The usual classroom difficulties are pretty minor affairs for teachers and students alike (Wragg, R5, 1984, p. 38).

For a down-to-earth pamphlet on discipline, see Farley's book *Your Discipline in School* (R2). A useful table appears in it which is reproduced on p. 84 (Table 5.1). It provides a number of the more difficult misdemeanours and gives advice on how these might be tackled (P4, p. 86).

Most reprimands are directed at undue noise. At the other extreme, one finds acts of vandalism, personal violence and other serious infringements of the law. In these cases, do not hesitate – consult with a senior member of staff or the head teacher. You may be able to help in identifying the causes, but this should be done in collaboration with a senior person in the school. The help of parents can sometimes be enlisted. Very occasionally, a child may be in need of psychological help (e.g. for emotional deviance) or counselling, for which the school should seek professional advice.

There will, of course, always be a few bright sparks who seek other kinds of stimulation and enjoyment from teacher baiting. They generally like attention and seem impervious to discipline – in fact, they may thrive on the attention which disciplining gives them. How can they be controlled? One school of thought with its roots in behaviourism (*PAT*, Chapter 5) has recently come to prominence in Britain; its motto, 'accentuate the positive', has been developed into a course of training for teachers (Wheldall and Merrett, R9).

Both American (for example, White, R10) and British (Merrett and Wheldall, R9) literature concludes that most teachers do *not* use approval as much as they believe they do, and very few use systematic methods of showing approval. Yet most teachers admit that praise works. A system devised by Wheldall and Merrett (R11), called the BATPACK (Behavioural Approach to Teaching Package), attempts to introduce teachers to a systematic programme of reinforcing behaviour in the classroom by improving their skills in behavioural analysis and management (D3, p. 86).

The BATPACK course requires 6 one-hour sessions and 'homework'. The sessions cover an introduction to the application of behavioural analysis in teaching, looking at and for good behaviour, practising and using positive reinforcement, getting the right setting for behaviour, and dealing with more difficult behaviour. The use of praise is particularly emphasised, alongside deliberate 'ignoring' of unacceptable behaviour (so as not to reward the child who is seeking attention at any price).

[BATPACK] concentrates upon improving the teacher's ability to manage the classroom situation as a whole rather than the behavioural/learning problems of particular children. It attempts to do this by helping teachers define clearly the commonest classroom behaviour problems and to observe them carefully, whilst concentrating upon positive measures to bring about change. BATPACK attempts to change teachers' responses to their classes principally by skilful attention to antecedents and by being more positive towards specifically defined child behaviours which they wish to encourage. [Wheldall and Merrett, R12, pp. 159–160]

PRACTICE AND OBSERVATION ACTIVITIES

P4   Look at the list of misdemeanours in Table 5.1, reproduced from Farley's book. Examine your own techniques against those recommended.

DISCUSSION AND ANALYSIS ACTIVITIES

D3   Read the work of Wheldall and Merrett (R12) on the BATPACK. Explore the possibilities of setting up a course and an enquiry into the merits of this approach to class disruption.

See also *PAT* for further information on applied behavioural analysis (Chapter 5, pp. 101–103). The results of trials with this system are encouraging. In primary schools, there was increased positive reward-giving behaviour by teachers in the experimental group and a corresponding increase in on-task work by their pupils.

TEACHER STYLES – ORGANISATIONAL STRATEGIES

Two detailed pieces of research have been conducted in this country in the last ten years which have explored the question of teachers' classroom organisational strategies. These have been classified into 'styles'. The research is described in Bennett, *Teaching Styles and Pupil Progress* (R13) and in a series of books relating to the ORACLE research at Leicester (Observational Research and Classroom Learning Evaluation) (see Galton and Simon; Galton, Simon and Croll, R14). The research is also mentioned in *PAT*, Chapter 10 (D4, p. 90).

Organisational strategy is defined by these researchers in the questions and observations they make. These cover the use of time, space, human and material resources in order to increase the efficiency of teaching and to maximise the opportunities offered to learners. They consider such questions as how long does a teacher spend on particular topics, transition frequency and time between different parts of lessons; how often is a pupil or group of pupils seen; how are children grouped – if at all; how long are they taught as a class; how is the class distributed; how are the desks arranged; are there mixed or selected ability groups, single or mixed sex classes; how much movement around the classroom is allowed; 'hands up if you want to speak', are children allowed to speak – when?

The important conclusion from this research is that managerial stereotypes emerge, and some idea of the relative performance of pupils has been gauged in various regimes. Both research studies mentioned above were carried out in primary schools. Whether these stereotypes are acquired as a result of teaching experience, whether they are pretty well established before a person begins to teach, or whether these stereotypes exist in secondary schools is still a matter for investigation. Nevertheless, some knowledge of the characteristics should prove useful to students, in order to become informed of possibilities into which their own strategies can fit and be tested.

Before elaborating on these various styles, however, it is important to note that most workers in the field accept the interaction effects of pupil and teacher behaviours, and that these in turn affect the performance of children. In other words, it is not just the teacher's 'transmission' strategies, but the pupil's 'reception' strategies which influence pupil performance. Bennett and the ORACLE team set out to answer, amongst other things, the question as to what extent teaching styles interact with pupil characteristics in order to produce differential outcomes.

Twelve teacher types in the form of a continuum were defined in Bennett's work. At the extremes we find Type 1:

> Teachers who favour integration of subject matter and, unlike most other groups, allow pupils choice of work, whether undertaken individually or in groups. Most allow pupils choice of seating. Less than half curb movement and talk. Assessment in all its forms – tests, grading, and homework – appears to be discouraged. Intrinsic motivation is favoured.

and Type 12:

> This is an extreme group in a number of respects. None favours an integrated approach. Subjects are taught separately by class teaching and individual work. None allows pupils choice of seating, and every teacher curbs movement and talk. These teachers are above average on all assessment procedures, and extrinsic motivation predominates.

These extremes suggest to Bennett an informal–formal continuum. A further important finding was a strong relationship between a teacher's aims and opinions and the way teachers actually teach.

The Bennett research also looked at the performance differences under the two extreme regimes of formal and informal. The results showed that in mathematics and English, pupils in the formal teachers' classrooms progress more than in mixed or informal classrooms. In reading, the pupils in the formal and mixed progressed more than those in the informal arrangement. However, this latter finding has come in for considerable criticism on statistical grounds and should be treated with some caution (*PAT*, Chapter 11).

The questions used by Bennett in deriving a classification of styles largely related to organisational strategies. In the ORACLE study, three aspects of teaching strategies were examined. In addition to the *organisational* strategies, the ORACLE team also looked at *curricular* and *instructional* strategies. They defined curricular strategies as dealing with the content and balance of the curriculum operated by a teacher within the classroom (not at 'school' level). Instructional strategies deal, as we have seen, with methods of teaching – lecture method, practical demonstration, questioning, pupils' involvement in practical work, projects, work cards, etc. In defining teaching styles, the ORACLE team used observation schedules.

Their analyses give rise to four *types* or *styles*, but one style had three manifestations, giving six in all. It is instructive to say a little about these

yles, because they differ in several respects from Bennett's, but, more
nportantly, they act as markers for self-observation and analysis for the
:udent-teacher.

The four styles were *individual monitors, class enquirers, group
instructors* and *style changers*. The latter divided into *infrequent
changers, rotating changers* and *habitual changers* (see *PAT*, for a more
etailed description of these styles, R13).

No direct correlation was found between these styles and the
ormal–informal unidimension of Bennett. Nevertheless, the ORACLE
eam carried out the same kind of analysis between these styles and
erformance differences in mathematics, English and reading. 'No
verall best style emerges from all three tests. While the *class enquirers*
were most successful in mathematics and language skills, it is the pupils
f the *infrequent changers* who make the greatest gains in reading.
However, in language skills the *class enquirers* enjoyed no over-all
uperiority from either the *group instructors* or the *infrequent changers*.
n mathematics the progress of pupils taught by *infrequent changers* did
iot differ significantly from that achieved by the group taught by *class
enquirers*.' (Galton and Simon, R14, p. 71).

Two results to notice are that the *rotating changers* have the least
uccessful style and the *class enquirers* tended to be the most successful in
nathematics.

Rotating changers are those who have children grouped in curriculum
ireas (English, maths, etc.), with each child often doing different tasks.
At intervals the groups of children would be asked to change curriculum
irea. It is not surprising that such a technique is unsuccessful. Teachers
iave difficulty talking to every child in a group. Children do not stay on
he task for as long as those involved in other strategies, presumably
because they cannot be monitored as efficiently. Interruption resulting
from the 'all change' strategy probably upsets the child who likes to
work alone.

Several studies (see review by Anthony, R15) suggest a link between
effective mathematics performance and *class* rather than *individual*
eaching. This is confirmed by Galton and Simon (R14), in that the
strategy of *class enquirer*, who spends a large proportion of time on class
eaching, gave rise to the largest pupil gains in mathematics.

> In the face of evidence from this [ORACLE] result and from other studies
> listed by Anthony, all using different methodologies and covering a period
> of nearly twenty years, it must be concluded that there is something about
> an approach based on class teaching which is helpful in getting pupils to
> solve mathematical problems of the type represented by traditional
> standardized tests. [Galton and Simon, R14, p. 72]

Two elements in organisational strategy which are a significant part of contemporary education are mixed ability classes, and the methods adopted by a teacher within a class for the grouping of children. Both these are discussed in the above studies, but for a thorough introduction students are advised to read a basic text such as Cohen and Manion (R16), where there is a chapter on mixed ability teaching which gives a good grounding (D5).

DISCUSSION AND ANALYSIS ACTIVITIES

D4 The area of teaching styles is a complex one and is a current source of research interest. It might pay for the tutorial group to look in detail at the questionnaires designed for the Bennett and ORACLE studies in order to discover the sorts of issues which lie behind the findings.

D5 Read Chapter 7 of L. Cohen and L. Manion, *Perspectives in Classrooms and Schools* (R16). There are several Enquiry and Discussion suggestions to look at. However, note in particular those aspects of mixed ability classes and grouping strategies you have experienced and look at them in terms of the age, subject and efficiency of the arrangements. What demands do they place on teachers? What do you believe are their effects on pupils' task performance?

TEACHER EXPECTATIONS

Management of the learning environment can be affected by subconscious as well as conscious attitudes and behaviours. One important influence is teacher expectancy, and sufficient evidence has now been gathered to show that pupil performance can sometimes be influenced by teachers' expectations (*PAT*, Chapter 3). Rogers (R17) suggests from the evidence gathered so far that *social expectations* held by teachers (to do with the behaviour and 'grooming' of children – the well-behaved and better-groomed child being favoured) are the ones more likely to have a determining effect on later academic performance than *academic expectations* (the pupil's perceived academic ability). This seems particularly true in the earlier stages of a child's school life than further up the system. Academic expectations are more likely to be the *outcome* of pupil performance than the *determiner* of it.

Another key influence involves the pressures bearing on teachers as a result of the circumstances in which they have to work. These help to form and shape expectations. The more a system conspires to distance the teacher from pupils, the more likely it is that teacher-expectancy effects will play a part in influencing pupil performance. Rogers (R17) lists a number of factors that create differential pressures on teachers and that, in turn, creates different sorts of 'distancing' between teacher and taught. Examples of such factors are type of school (urban/rural; inner city/middle-class suburban), resource levels, pupil–teacher ratios, degree of support from the local community, status of teachers in society (and the effect this has on morale) and inter-staff relationships in the school (D6, p. 91).

Rogers gives a most useful summary to his review of research in this field which students should look at carefully:

> We can tentatively state that teacher-expectancy effects are likely to occur (but certainly not exclusively so) when younger pupils are involved, when teachers have formed social expectations for their pupils under conditions likely to lead to the establishment of relatively distant teacher–pupil relationships and under conditions (as yet largely unspecified) where the actions and expressed attitudes of the teacher are most likely to affect pupils' level of motivation and self-concepts. [Rogers, R17, p. 172]

DISCUSSION AND ANALYSIS ACTIVITIES

D6   The whole question of teacher expectancy and its effect on pupil performance is still a matter for cautious comment. Look at the factors suggested by Rogers (R17) and reproduced above which are said to create pressures on teachers and thus affect the relationships with children. Look back at these and discuss them in relation to your own experiences, both as a pupil and in the school already visited as a student.

ADVICE TO PARENTS – MANAGEMENT OF STUDY AT HOME

For a beginning teacher, one of the most daunting tasks is having to face the parents of pupils. This happens formally at parent/teacher meetings organised by the school or when parents are invited to come to the school for a discussion about the progress of their children. There are, of course, informal gatherings and meetings (sports days, when parents request a meeting with teachers), or when the school asks parents to

come for a discussion about a particular matter (career, serious mis
conduct).

Why is it important to meet pupils' parents? One of the mos
perceptive quotations I have read recently appears in Goacher and Rei
(R18), in which a teacher crystallises out a number of important reason
and uses for discussion with parents. They enable:

> teachers to make a much fuller report than is possible in writing: answer
> queries that arise, and engage in a meaningful dialogue with parents so
> that any problems may be clarified and tackled jointly. Teachers can also
> gain much from meeting the parents and in a conversation it is possible to
> assess how much information/criticism can be transmitted: it is also
> possible to learn about the home background, the amount of support one
> can expect, e.g. *re* dress, homework and the like. The student's problems
> can also be discussed in greater detail, and often one evokes a greater
> degree of empathy – and sympathy – from these meetings. The students
> feel that they are important as individuals, not merely ciphers, or one of a
> class. Parents can assess the attitude of teachers; clarify misunder-
> standings, e.g. ambiguity in reports; discover the areas where the child
> needs most help; avoid or reduce tension/personality clashes and request
> changes. Pupils also recognise that (in the main) parents and teachers are
> co-operating in the education of the children. [Goacher and Reid, R18,
> p. 111]

One particular kind of advice which teachers might be able to offe
relates to working at home (P5, p. 96). This aspect of school lif
increases in importance when the pupil moves into middle and secondary
education, although work is set for exploration in primary-aged pupils
As the pupil reaches the age of public examinations, homework loom
even larger and parents have a responsibility to provide suitabl
conditions.

For parents

Students and teachers might find what follows a helpful way o
approaching parents who are anxious to help their children, particularly
in preparation for examinations (R19). Most parents will have taken an
exam or test at some time. Driving tests are probably the most common.
Those who have taken a driving test will recall the moments of anxiety in
the days before the test, those feelings of 'butterflies', while pondering
about what on earth the examiner will ask from the Highway Code.
Imagine that experience extended over three or four weeks with several
different subjects, each demanding much more than a Highway Code,
and you begin to capture the feelings children endure when preparing for
and taking public examinations.

Studying for homework or an examination is hard work, if done properly. Parents cannot do the learning for their offspring, but there are several ways in which they can provide much needed understanding and support. They do not have to know anything about the subjects being studied, but what they have to do is provide the right atmosphere for study.

Teachers, when advising parents, should make the point that there are some obvious questions for parents to ask themselves. Can their sons and daughters get peace and quiet in the home when they need it? Can they provide space, reasonable comfort and warmth? Is there a reasonable table top and book space? Do they fork out when books or equipment are needed? Do they lay on the odd drink (non-alcoholic, as alcohol befuddles the mind) or snack during periods of intensive study? Are the students relieved from some routine household chores (but not all, because they should break from time to time for alternative activities)?

The important contribution of parents is really to provide support services and sympathy, *without* bringing undue pressure to bear. Many parents understandably get worried and anxious for their children's sakes, largely because parents realise the high value our society places on examination successes and the place these successes have in the career prospects of young people. Tempting though it may be to make regular enquiries about how things are going, they should try not to overdo it – they should try to avoid becoming a nagging parent. Equally, they must not ignore the activities and progress of their young. There is a responsible middle course, which is extremely difficult to steer, between the overbearing and the passive. In effect, they have to believe in their children; they must have faith in them and build up a trust in them.

Perhaps the hardest problem to deal with is the able, but lazy, son or daughter. How, for example, does a caring parent encourage an able, bone-idle youth to work without the parent 'laying on the agony'? Two major sources of trouble are lack of motivation and a troublesome personality.

To be an effective student one has to want to do well. There are so many appealing distractions for young people that the alternative of sitting for long hours pouring over books or notes has to have a strong justification. The temptation to leave school for a wage is powerful, and the central discussion will doubtless be about putting off moderate, short-term satisfactions in favour of better, more rewarding and satisfying career prospects in the future. It is not easy to convince young people that longer-term rewards are worth working and waiting for. Other factors are that immediate satisfaction is usually possible when some of the subjects being studied are of genuine interest, or when they come easily to the individual. Sometimes subjects are essential for a particular career. Extrinsic rewards for success in exams can be offered – for instance, a promise of money, a bicycle, the cost of driving lessons, a holiday and so forth, as the occasion demands.

Something is said in *PAT* (Chapter 11, pp. 253–254) about the possible effect of certain personality traits on study. Some people do find the act of studying for prolonged periods very tedious. They have to recognise and come to terms with this disadvantage and adjust their study plans so that the periods are interspersed. Some frank discussion between parents and offspring about these difficulties can be helpful.

Teachers should make it clear that if parents are to provide support, they need to be informed of the school's expectations. It is not a bad idea to obtain from their youngsters some outline of the homework timetable and talk through ways in which this can be achieved. Programmes for exam revision should also be shared with parents, so that they can give tactful encouragement when needed.

For pupils

This subsection is rather in the same spirit as Polonius's advice to his son (R18). If you have the ability to cope with the work done during the course and you have tried to keep level with your understanding of the work, how could you possibly fail? Unfortunately, people do fail, even when they have enough ability to come to terms with the course. Why? There are several reasons, but one of the most important is that you have to be 'motivated', that is, you have to feel a need to get through the exams. If you have a definite career in mind, keep it at the focus of your thoughts. There is nothing more potent than a goal which you want to attain. If you are half-hearted and unsure if you want to go on, it will not help at all. So you must try to get in the right frame of mind. You have to be convinced about the kind of future you want and the need to pass exams as well as you can.

Think twice before giving way to temptations which will squander your time away. The hours you need to put in are different and sometimes longer than those for your friends at work; so keep a close watch on the distribution of work and leisure time. Do not misunderstand this advice. Everyone should mix pleasure with work. But *you* have to be in control. You have to judge sensibly how much time you can afford for relaxation and when it is most convenient to take it. The decisions require a pretty tough and determined person.

Thus, look for pointers which will strengthen your desire to succeed

...d thereby help you overcome the many alternative temptations. If you ...ve a career in mind, work systematically towards it; where subjects ...terest you, work at them – almost like a hobby; take the advice of your ...achers when they tell you that you have skills in certain subjects. These ...n all be useful motivators.

Sometimes, and in all walks of life, we become despondent, impatient ...d tired of the routines. Study is no exception. It is work and work can ... boring at times. Some people, because of the way they react to life, ...nd they simply cannot keep up one task for even moderate periods of ...me. They soon switch off, even when they are well motivated. What can ... done? The first and most important thing is to recognise and face ...roblems and try to do something about them. It is not enough to admit ... oneself, and possibly others, that one cannot study for long. A regime ...as to be worked out which best suits one's shifts of mood.

In studying for exams, it should be emphasised that there is no one ...est method of studying. Broadly, there are ways and means which most ...eople find a help or a hindrance, but in the end pupils have to try out ...nd discover which combination of methods best suits their circum-...ances. Study guides are often written by those who have been success-...l in exams, and it becomes easy to slip into the habit of giving formulae ...r study which they have tried and proved effective.

Above all, pupils have to experiment and be honest with themselves. ...here is no future in their kidding themselves that they work brilliantly in ...range places at strange times without first confirming that there is no ...etter way. They should explore the most preferred *and* efficient tech-...iques in preparation for and in sitting exams. Some are common sense ...nd will be widely known, such as avoiding misreading questions or ...structions, writing so badly that the examiner cannot read the script or ...ot caring about the spelling of important concepts. Others are not so ...bvious, such as how should revision be spaced, judging the length of ...me which should be given to each subject, or whether to revise right up ... the exam or not.

Pupils need to use the normal school and 'mock' examinations as a ...uide to the best revision strategies, and use homework as a means of dis-...overing the most fruitful methods of study. They should treat any ...mock' exams very seriously, as if they were the real thing, and learn as ...uch as possible about their strengths and weaknesses.

It is important to get into the right frame of mind for examinations. ...thers are sure to say discouraging things about their prospects (and ...naybe yours as well). Take no notice – unless it is advice from a teacher ...f course. If there are those who claim not to need to work for exams, ...gnore them. They are probably working harder than you think. In any case, you should know best what you can do. One has to go into this business with a positive, optimistic outlook, knowing that if one has put in the work, success can be achieved. From the point of view of the future, taking 'O' levels, CSEs and 'A' levels is one of the most important events in a pupil's life so far. Treat the occasion with the care it deserves.

PRACTICE AND OBSERVATION ACTIVITIES

P5   Discuss with experienced teachers the strategies they use with parents at official parent/teacher meetings and unofficial meetings (when a parent comes to the school informally). What kinds of questions arise from parents? Do these vary with age and school? Are there opportunities to give advice about examination preparation support in the home for secondary-aged pupils?

REFERENCES

R1   J. Calderhead, *Teachers' Classroom Decision Making*, Holt, Rinehart and Winston, London, 1984.

R2   R. Farley, *Your Discipline in School*, New Education Press, London, 1984.

R3   M. Marland, *The Craft of the Classroom: a Survival Guide*, Heinemann Educational Books, London, 1975.

R4   W. J. Gnagey, *Maintaining Discipline in Classroom Instruction*, Macmillan, London, 1975.

R5   E. C. Wragg, *Class Management and Control*, Macmillan, London, 1981. E. C. Wragg (Ed.), *Classroom Teaching Skills*, Croom Helm, London, 1984.

R6   J. S. Kounin, *Discipline and Group Management in Classrooms*, Holt, Rinehart and Winston, New York, 1970. See *PAT*, Chapter 11.

R7   R. Lippitt and R. K. White, 'An experimental study of leadership and group life', in E. E. Maccoby, T. M. Newcomb and E. E. Hartley, *Readings in Social Psychology*, Holt, Rinehart and Winston, London, 1958. Leadership qualities: *PAT*, Chapter 11, pp. 259–262.

R8   P. Woods, *The Divided School*, Routledge and Kegan Paul, London, 1979. Survival strategies: *PAT*, Chapter 11.

R9   K. Wheldall and R. E. Merrett, *Positive Teaching. The Behavioural Approach*, Allen and Unwin, London, 1984. F. E. Merrett and K. Wheldall, 'Natural rates of teachers' approval and disapproval in primary and middle school classrooms', paper presented to the third annual conference of the Association for Behavioural Approaches with Children at Coventry, 1980.

R10 M. A. White, 'Natural rates of teacher approval and disapproval in the classroom', *Journal of Applied Behavioural Analysis*, **8**, 91–94 (1975).

R11 K. Wheldall and F. E. Merrett, 'The behavioural approach to classroom management', in D. Fontana, *Behaviourism and Learning Theory in Education*, Scottish Academic Press, Edinburgh, 1984. Also see *PAT*, Chapter 5.

R12 K. Wheldall and F. E. Merrett, 'Training teachers to be more positive: the behavioural approach', in N. Bennett and C. Desforges, *Recent Advances in Classroom Research*, Scottish Academic Press (published for the *British Journal of Educational Psychology*), Edinburgh, 1985.

R13 N. Bennett, *Teaching Styles and Pupil Progress*, Open Books, London, 1976. Teaching styles: *PAT*, Chapter 10, pp. 262–265.

R14 M. Galton, B. Simon and P. Croll, *Inside the Primary Classroom*, Routledge and Kegan Paul, London, 1980. M. Galton and B. Simon (Eds), *Progress and Performance in the Primary Classroom*, Routledge and Kegan Paul, London, 1980.

R15 W. S. Anthony, 'Progressive learning theories: the evidence', in G. Bernbaum (Ed.), *Schooling in Decline*, Macmillan, London, 1979.

R16 L. Cohen and L. Manion, *Perspectives in Classrooms and Schools*, Holt, Rinehart and Winston, London, 1981.

R17 C. Rogers, *A Social Psychology of Schooling: the Expectancy Process*, Routledge and Kegan Paul, London, 1982.

R18 B. Goacher and M. I. Reid, *School Reports to Parents*, NFER–Nelson, Windsor, 1983.

R19 Study: *PAT*, Chapter 6, pp. 125–133.

6

Assessment and Evaluation of Learning and Teaching

Two of the most important activities for teachers are assessing the progress of pupils and evaluating the effectiveness of their own teaching. Without some positive effort to monitor the success or otherwise of classroom learning experiences, there would be neglect of an important responsibility in our educational system. One purpose of formal schooling is to speed up the process of assimilating useful knowledge and experience about our world in order to enable the next generation to benefit from the experiences of previous ones at a pace which is well beyond that which could be expected from normal life-chances. It is better to face these classroom judgements with some idea of their limitations.

This chapter is divided into two sections. The first deals with aspects of assessment of performance of pupils and the evaluation of that performance. The second looks at a schedule for the teacher's self-assessment and evaluation of teaching effectiveness.

ASSESSMENT OF LEARNING

Why do we need to assess learning and how do we discover if it has taken place? These questions are frequently regarded by some as contentious. Despite this, teachers continue to view assessment as an important part of their work (P1, p. 103). The reasons are discussed in most texts on the subject (see *PAT*, Chapter 13). In summary, teachers need to know something about pupils' attainment because parents, other teachers, education authorities, employers and other institutions to which a pupil is transferring want to know. The pupils also like to know how they are progressing. Diagnosis of difficulties or consistent errors, the evaluation of standards or content (e.g. national surveys, NFER tests, assessment

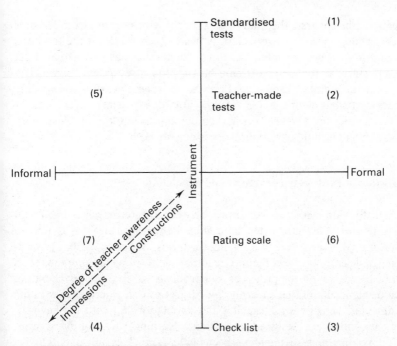

Figure 6.1 A classification of classroom assessment practices. From D. Satterly, *Assessment in Schools*, p. 13, Basil Blackwell, Oxford, 1981. Reproduced with permission.

of performance in various school subjects), and both formative and summative feedback are not possible without some form of assessment.

The form (the *how*) of assessment varies considerably according to circumstances, but Satterly (R1) gives a useful summary adapted in Figure 6.1. The vertical line labelled 'instrument' relates to the particular form of presentation used, whether it be a published standardised test, home-made teacher test through to simple check lists (e.g. list of spellings, ten snappy arithmetic questions with simple answers). Teachers will recognise all these methods. The second, horizontal dimension distinguishes informal–formal assessments. Informal assessments are very frequently made by teachers, particularly in formative judgements during normal class learning. On the other hand, formal judgements tend to be made at times set aside specifically for the purpose of testing (e.g. examinations). The third dimension, running at right-angles to the other two (not possible to draw on a flat page!), tries to account for the varying degrees of conscious, deliberate teacher awareness of the judgements made using well-constructed assessment situations. This useful dimension is defined by Satterly (R1). At one extreme he suggests the kind of assessment which results from features of a child's performance which . . . "leave their mark on the teacher's mind" ', but are not intentional until the teacher has to make a verbal comment. At the other extreme he suggests assessments 'in which a teacher deliberately used pre-set criteria and where he or she is explicitly aware of what he or she was "looking for" '. Figure 6.1 covers most of the methods used by teachers in their day-to-day work in the classroom. More will be said later about the various methods.

Distinction between assessment and evaluation

A distinction needs to be drawn between the terms *assessment* and *evaluation*. They are often used interchangeably, but this is not an accurate or useful way of applying the terms. Satterly (R1, p. 3) distinguishes clearly between them. For him, *assessment* is 'an omnibus term which includes all the processes and products which describe the nature and extent of children's learning, its degree of correspondence with the aims and objectives of teaching and its relationship with the environments which are designed to facilitate learning'. *Evaluation* is what follows once an assessment has been made. It involves judgements about the effectiveness and worth of something for which the assessment has already been made – usually a teaching objective. One would assess the level of performance of a child in a given topic, but these results would be used to examine the suitability of the material for that child – that is, evaluation.

RANGE OF ASSESSMENT METHODS

Having lived through the educational system, student-teachers reading this book will be familiar with a wide variety of assessment procedures (D1, p. 103). In the nursery and primary school, we experience 'on the spot' tests of knowledge and skill, with the occasional reading, writing or number test. We may even have experienced taking an ability test or been part of a national survey. Sometimes the teacher makes a mental note of achievement (the impressions end of the 'teacher awareness' dimension of Figure 6.1), as a result of class discussion or question and answer sessions; at other times tests with 'norms' are given. In the secondary school, formal testing becomes more and more likely the older one gets. Thus, at the end of term, teacher-set examinations and public examinations for CSE or GCE 'O' and 'A' level loom large.

One way of defining the wide range of assessment methods is to classify them according to what is used as the means of making judgements about performance. The question is what reference points are used? The two commonest sources of judgement are either *norms* or *specified criteria*, and the ensuing tests are called *norm-referenced* and *criterion-referenced* tests (R2, R1).

Norm-referenced tests

The important feature of norm-referencing, as the term implies, is the use of the performance of others who have taken the test under controlled conditions in order to make an assessment of an individual's performance in relation to those others – how 'normal' is the individual's score compared with others. Fundamentally, norm-referencing has to do with discriminating between individuals in a group by comparing all their scores. Often these discriminations are converted into words and phrases along a rough scale, from very poor, poor, average, good, very good, excellent, or synonyms for these. It is very tempting and not unreasonable for teachers to compare the standing of a child with that of others in the same age and/or abilities range.

Some examples of norm-referencing in schools will be recognised by the reader (R3). Some schools have a policy of converting marks to percentages and banding these, sometimes as literal grades A to E or F, sometimes as standard comments which reflect performance above, at or below average. Public examinations such as 'O' and 'A' levels are based on trends in performance from year to year by large numbers of pupils. Primary and middle schools often give children reading tests from which a 'reading age' is obtained. This age is worked out using the performance statistics of many youngsters of a similar age. Competence is expressed in terms of the age-level at which the child is performing. This may then be compared with the child's chronological age (R4). If Jane is 8 years and 3 months and her reading age is 10 years and 1 month, then she is a bright, exceptionally good reader. Intelligence tests are also based on norms derived from sampling and comparing large numbers of people (R2).

Criterion-referencing

Ideally, every teacher might hope that at the end of a lesson all her/his pupils will achieve complete mastery of the work presented. In reality, one finds a whole range of different levels of achievement for a task. Individual differences in performance arise from many causes. Some children have insufficient grasp of the ground work to enable understanding of the task in hand; some children might have difficulty with the conceptual demands of the task; some children have not tried; others need more time to achieve a high percentage of mastery. There are many other causes. Where the emphasis is upon testing whether the child has reached a particular goal or criterion, regardless of the performance of others, it is said to be 'criterion-referenced'. A task is set and sufficient time is given to the child to reach a predetermined level of performance. The child's performance is said to be interpreted without reference to that of others. For example, suppose we had given a series of lessons on 'significant figures' expressed either as numbers or decimals and we wanted to test how well the pupils could cope. Several problems would be set at chosen levels of difficulty, bringing out various awkward issues. For example, express the following to two significant figures: 0.007 614, 0.012 91, 3.7849, 65 513.2 (the answers would be 0.0076, 0.013, 3.8, 66 000). The first of these four problems would demonstrate the pupil's grasp of the basic concept that two *figures* only must appear in the answer (i.e. 76). The second problem above is a little more difficult, because the third number is greater than 4, thus one is added to the next figure, 2, for an approximation to two significant figures (i.e. the answer becomes 13). The third gets even more complicated, because it involves whole numbers in the decimal *and* the third number is greater than 4, so to seven we add one. Finally, the fourth illustrates the position with whole numbers and decimals. There is a gradual increase in complexity. A teacher wishing to test out whether pupils had overcome the various pitfalls would set several problems in each kind and also set a criterion of mastery. Frequently 80 per cent correct answers is used. A child with, for example, ten problems of the first kind would be expected to get 8 right to give evidence of mastery.

We can use this example to demonstrate one difference between norm- and criterion-referencing. If Mary got 7 out of 10 and the average for her class was, say, 6, she would be regarded as better than average – above the norm. However, using the criterion of 8 out of 10, she has *not* been successful and would need to practise until she could achieve this level. Striving for and reaching a specified criterion is sometimes referred to as *mastery learning* (R5). The length of time needed to reach the level is less important than achieving it. This is both a strength and a weakness. Children generally work at different speeds and this should be allowed for in their progress through a topic. However, school life is short and there is so much to be achieved in the time. It might be argued by some that a child cannot be given all the time in the world to master each step. Teachers might have to settle for somewhat less than 80 per cent competence in order to do all the other things in a busy school day.

PRACTICE AND OBSERVATION ACTIVITIES

P1   Assessment is such a vital part of the teacher's task that you should explore on school observation *all* the methods used in the schools you visit. Ask questions about the reliability of the assessments used. Compare and contrast methods at different ages and ability levels.

DISCUSSION AND ANALYSIS ACTIVITIES

D1   The variety of assessment methods available, their close examination, practice in their use (where appropriate) and critical appraisal of the outcomes are essential. All parts of your training course will generally make a contribution to this aspect of your work as a teacher. Satterly's book (R1) will give you a sound basis in the topic.

Another point worth noting about norm- and criterion-referencing is that they are interrelated. It is not possible to have the latter without the former. Deciding on the topics to take with a particular class has an element of norm-referencing, that is, deciding what is normal for a group of children at a given age. Also, in settling for 80 per cent success rate (or any other level), there is an assumption that mastery is 'normally' achieved at that level.

PURPOSES OF ASSESSMENT IN SCHOOLS

Having discussed the two dominant modes of assessment for the measurement of performance, norm- and criterion-referenced tests, which aim to fulfil different functions, we turn to the questions of the purposes for which and for whom assessments are made.

The list below gives a pen-picture of the main purposes for which assessment takes place:

Type of assessment	*Purpose*
1. Pretask	To discover the knowledge and skills possessed by someone before embarking on a learning task
2. Formative	To assess the progress and development of knowledge and skills during the process of learning
3. Diagnostic/remedial	To locate particular difficulties in the acquisition or application of knowledge and skills
4. Summative	To measure the outcomes of learning

Those who are most interested in the information provided by assessments are the learners, the teachers and others outside the classroom who need to know the competence or progress of the pupils. The pupils probably gain most from formative and diagnostic analysis, because these assessments are built in such a way as to be valuable for feedback to the pupils. Summative assessment, most frequently applied at the end of a topic or course, is not usually analysed for feedback, but used as an estimate of knowledge and skills learned in readiness for further applications. Clearly this kind of information is useful for parents, employers, other institutions (next school, university) or teachers (next class). Teachers make use of all four types of assessment. In this section we shall look a little more closely at these purposes, and in the next section we shall combine the sections dealt with so far in looking at some examples of classroom assessment.

In *pretask assessment* the teacher is concerned to discover the knowledge base from which subsequent lessons can take off. Students just beginning their teaching practice with unknown pupils are rightly worried about the level at which to pitch the lesson topics allocated. In most cases they are advised by the teacher who normally takes the classes. Occasionally it is necessary to devise a pretest. A new class at the beginning of the school year is sometimes questioned before the serious business of planning begins. Experienced teachers who are familiar with the age-groups they inherit tend not to need to be cold blooded in their pursuit of this information; they have seen it all before! But it is wise for the inexperienced to build up a firm knowledge of each child's incoming competence.

The methods used range from informal, almost casual, to standardised tests (see the 'instrument' dimension of Figure 6.1). A few question and answer sessions at the beginning of the academic year with those pupils not seen before is often used. As well as oral questioning, the early work of new pupils is examined for consistent errors or omissions. Teachers' home-made tests are sometimes used, often designed from previous experience, to find the range of talent amongst the pupils. Less frequently, standardised tests are employed; reading and number tests, for example, from the National Foundation for Educational Research (NFER) are sometimes given to new entrants to lower junior school. At transfer to middle, or more particularly secondary school, standardised ability tests in general intelligence, number and English are used. Some authorities still retain the 11 + entry examination as a 'pretask' mechanism by which to predict the most advantageous educational provision according to ability.

Formative assessment (also referred to as formative evaluation, but it is frequently employed as an assessment) takes place during the process of instruction and is used to guide, evaluate, feed back information to pupils and estimate the effectiveness of teaching. Most of the teacher's assessment effort is taken up in this way. Again, a whole range of instruments from informal check lists to standardised diagnostic tests are used for this purpose. Of all the forms of assessment referred to above, children are supposed to benefit from the most formative methods. The intention is to optimise feedback to pupils, pointing out strengths and weaknesses, and guiding their subsequent work. This strategy, however, equally applies to the teacher. His/her schemes are subject to modification in the light of lessons learned from pupil responses. The essential idea of formative assessment is to obtain information by which to modify and improve a programme of work.

Diagnostic assessment is crucial when you wish to provide help and guidance to individual pupils who have difficulty with particular aspects of work. It arises with the formative assessment period, when children are displaying problems. Again, the range of methods used stretches from informal analysis to standardised methods using specific tools designed to pinpoint the sources of difficulty.

Finally, *summative assessment* takes place at the end of the process of instruction and is used to discover the effectiveness of learning. It is rarely used to analyse difficulties (although one might learn from the mistakes in readiness for a repeat assessment, if this is available). A driving test, CSE, GCE, 'O' and 'A' levels, end-of-term examinations in primary and secondary schools are examples. The outcome of these assessments is most often used by those outside the classroom. As is well known to the reader, CSE and GCE results are used not only as measures of learning achieved, but as predictors of future performance (not always in comparable situations, such as industry). End-of-term exams are one well-used means of summarising the competence of pupils, although reports these days also contain other kinds of evaluation of work during the year (see later) (P2, p. 111).

SOME EXAMPLES OF INSTRUMENTS FOR ASSESSMENT

A comprehensive literature has built up over the years on the design and extent of assessment instruments and it is not intended to repeat this here (D2, p. 111). Reference R6 contains a number of books which I hope the reader will find not only useful, but readable. The basic question facing every teacher is *why* do I want to make an assessment? *What* purpose will it serve? Considerable assessment of a crude, unreliable kind takes place every hour in the classroom. As human beings, we spend a lot of our lives weighing up other human beings on the flimsiest of evidence. Provided we are not going to use the outcome of such subjective analyses as a means of influencing another person's life-chances, it might be excused. But in this day and age, when accountability and exam-oriented education is uppermost in the minds of society, it is absolutely essential that we make sure our judgements are based on the firmest evidence we can muster. The risk is that we spend too much time assessing and not enough time guiding the learning process. Teachers have a tremendous responsibility to find the sensible balance between these two functions of learning and of assessing what is learned.

Figure 6.1 is a good starting point for drawing up a range of examples of instruments which can be used by the teacher. The 'instrument' dimension starts at the bottom with 'check lists' (D3, p. 111). Of course there are methods not included on this dimension, several of which have been mentioned above. Feedback from question and answer sessions with the children, simple class tests, exercises at the latter part of lessons are very popular, indeed essential, and they all contribute to our picture of a child's competence, but we must be aware of their levels of reliability and validity.

What is a *check list*? It is a list of activities, steps in a problem, which attempts to give a systematic progression. A child can ('yes') or cannot ('no') carry out a particular step in the list. The criterion-referencing mentioned earlier can be assessed using this method. It rests upon the ability of teachers to break down a procedure into sufficiently small and recognisable steps for an observation schedule to be drawn up, which is *not* an easy task. Try breaking down the steps in solving a problem set earlier: 'express 0.007 614 to two significant figures'.

(a)   Does the child understand decimals?
(b)   Does the child understand places of decimals?
(c)   What is a significant figure?
(d)   Are zeros significant *figures*?
(e)   What happens to the other figures?

Careful analysis of errors is required to get at the root of pupils' difficulties in solving such a problem.

Profile reports frequently contain check lists, as we shall see later. An example is given below relating to secondary-school language skills. Each question requires a yes/no response.

(a)   Has legible handwriting.
(b)   Can write simple sentences.
(c)   Can read and understand a popular newspaper.
(d)   Can use simple punctuation correctly.
(e)   Avoids elementary spelling mistakes.
(f)   Can write a personal letter.
(g)   Can give and take a telephone message.
(h)   Can accurately complete a passport application.
(i)   Regularly borrows from school or public library.
(j)   Can write a business letter.
(k)   Can make an accurate written report.
(l)   Can make a clear spoken report.
(m)   Can summarise accurately a notice or report.
(n)   Can understand simple instructions in a foreign language.
(o)   Can give a simple instruction in a foreign language.

Rating scales are slightly more sophisticated than the check list alluded to above. Ratings are generally classified in graduations from one extreme to another, e.g. very good—very poor; easy—hard. Another example from a profile record used by a school for personal assessment is given below:

Qualities	*Rating*
Standard of work presentation	
Perseverance in completing a task	
Making most of his/her ability	
Ability to work without supervision	
Initiative	
Etc.	

The rating is (1) very good; (2) good; (3) average; (4) poor; (5) very poor. Again 'school effort' is frequently recorded in terms of grades: (1) excellent; (2) good; (3) satisfactory; (4) unsatisfactory; (5) poor.

Teacher-made tests are the most used of all the instruments mentioned. Books have been written on this subject, and summaries can be found below (R6). All the purposes for which assessments are applied by teachers can be met using teacher-made tests. The problem is often that teachers have neither the time not the resources to design thorough-going 'reliable' and 'valid' tests, and must settle for something less high powered. Often, the teacher needs something specific to the particular part of the curriculum, involving extensive sampling of a small section of work or testing out known problems which the pupils have, and these are better achieved using home-made tests. The difference between a standardised test and one devised the night before it is to be given can be tremendous. It is therefore wise to bear in mind the normal procedures of test construction when thinking up a test. At least bear in mind the following points:

(a) Do you know why you are testing? Have this clear from the start. Is it pretask, formative, diagnostic, summative?

(b) Plan out the areas to be tested and the number of questions required in each area.

(c) If the test is diagnostic you will need sufficient items in each skill area to make sure you have covered all the possibilities. Some test designers reckon you should have at least ten items in each sub-area.

(d) Carefully consider the level of difficulty of the items. There should be a range of difficulty, with most questions being of average difficulty and just a sprinkling of very hard or easy ones.

Teachers will continue to use 'quickies' where, say, ten specific problems are given to test the extent of learning in a particular lesson, and this kind of assessment has an important place as part of the revision process. But the teacher must still have very clearly in mind why the test has been set, what level of competence is demanded, how the results could be used. More serious assessment such as end-of-term or public examinations or diagnostic testing deserve careful planning and analysis, and reference has already been made to several texts which contain details of the various kinds of subjective or objective test designs (R6). Frequently this part of a teacher's responsibilities are left too much to chance; training institutions should ensure that potential teachers have all the necessary knowledge and skills to carry out a valid and reliable assessment of pupil work.

Sometimes it is possible to obtain a well-tried *standardised test* from a reputable source which has been carefully designed for a particular purpose and for which useful statistics are provided. For example, some standardised tests have a range of mean scores for given age-groups, or an 'age' can be calculated such as 'reading', 'number' or 'mental' ages. These give a performance yardstick in terms of the age-level at which a child is performing on the test, i.e. a child whose 'reading age' is eight years is characteristically reading like an 8-year-old child on the material provided – although his/her actual age could be anything within the range for which the test was designed.

Standardised tests are used principally for measuring ability, level of attainment or diagnosis, prediction and monitoring standards. In Britain the best established producer and distributor of standardised tests is the National Foundation for Educational Research (NFER). This organisation has produced many tests, some of which are available for use by teachers (R7). Other tests require specialist administration and analysis.

It will be useful to give some idea of the range of material available from the NFER. The pre-school and early education collection of tests includes assessment of weakness in conceptual development, pre-reading skills and screening for various forms of handicap. There are also 'intervention' programmes, used to improve the skills and to help in the teaching of slow-learning children (D2, p. 111). The general ability tests cover a wide range of verbal and non-verbal reasoning and spatial ability. Aptitude in modern languages and creativity tests are also available. Tests for those children with special needs include the Frostig developmental test of visual perception, comprehension, language imitation, reading and scales for the visually handicapped. For those in secondary school with responsibility or interest in vocational guidance and counselling, an extensive battery of inventories and tests exist. (A separate catalogue of tests for industry will also prove of interest to these teachers.)

The monitoring of standards has become a major activity of the Department of Education and Science, chiefly in the form of the Assessment of Performance Unit (APU). The DES programme, which extends back to the mid–1970s is concerned with the assessment of children's performance in selected school subjects at given ages between 10 and 15. Mathematics, English, science, modern languages are now well established, and the first three are entering a period in which standards will be tested at five-year intervals. For those teaching these subjects in upper junior, middle or secondary school, it would be advisable to read some of the literature. 'Occasional papers' are being published, which offer readable analyses of various aspects of the work (R8).

Ōne particularly instructive development from the mathematics programme is the *analysis of errors* (R9). Three very useful conclusions from these analyses are important for those students who will be teaching mathematics in primary, middle or secondary schools. The first is that children's errors seem to depend as much on *the way* a question is asked as on the mathematics involved. In one study, the same questions were posed in different ways, giving quite marked differences in response rates.

One example was:

			Percentage correct
1.	(a)	What is the square root of 16	76
	(b)	$\sqrt{16}$	71
	(c)	$16^{\frac{1}{2}}$	14

A second example was:

2.   (a)   Using the line *XY* as base, draw a rectangle which has the same area as shape *A*.

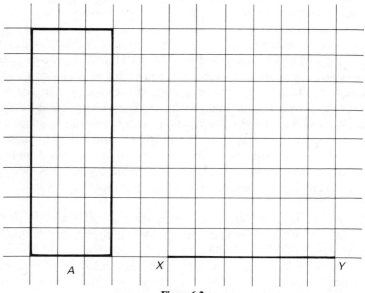

Figure 6.2

(b)   A rectangle has length 8 m and width 3 m. Another rectangle of the same area is drawn with length 6 m. What is its width?

(c)   A gardener has enough grass-seed to seed a lawn 8 m by 3 m. If, instead, he uses it to seed a lawn 6 m long, how wide will it be?

The response pattern for the second example was:

Question	Percentage correct (6 × 4)	*Percentage incorrect by preserving the perimeter*
(a)	76	2
(b)	60	11
(c)	51	24

The percentage of pupils getting the correct response gradually declines as the number choosing to preserve the perimeter increases. It can be concluded that the way a question is posed is a crucial determinant of success.

The second point to note is the key place of practical mathematics in helping pupils to think mathematically and gain confidence in the subject. For one thing verbal understanding does not intrude to the same extent and where there is a dialogue between the teacher and the pupil solving a practical problem, it is possible to give clues and hints. Payoff for the teacher comes in the form of greater understanding of how the child has arrived at solutions – presumably because of the closer collaboration in the problem-solving process. The Cockcroft Committee on Mathematics (R10) strongly supports the place of practical testing in enabling pupils and teachers to achieve methodical probing of responses.

The third point reiterates a well-known basic one of mathematics teaching that pupils must understand the logic of mathematical processes. Evidence from the APU research nevertheless suggests that much work presented in mathematics is based on incomplete understanding of earlier work essential for its understanding. Decimals offer a good

---

PRACTICE AND OBSERVATION ACTIVITIES

P2 While on teaching practice, discuss with teachers the range of assessment methods in use in the school. Examine your own assessment methods. Look at all these in terms of the four types of assessment mentioned in this chapter.

DISCUSSION AND ANALYSIS ACTIVITIES

D2 Read the suggested literature in R6 and the NFER documentation in R7. Piece together the findings from P2 above with the range of instruments available. Discuss the appropriate use of these instruments and comment on the methods you and those you have observed use.

D3 A number of instruments are mentioned in the text (e.g. check lists, rating scales, teacher-made tests, standardised tests, analysis of errors). Read the background literature, look at the tests available to teachers (e.g. NFER material). With the rest of the tutorial group, get as much practice as you can in the design, application and analysis of these tests.

example. Frequently children make errors because they do not really understand the basic consistencies which must govern the use of decimals. For example, there is often an inability to generalise from numbers greater than one to numbers less than one.

MARKING AND RECORDING

Marking

A time-consuming, but important, function of a teacher is marking work (D4, p. 113). In standardised or well-designed teacher-made tests, the marking system is carefully laid down beforehand. Public examinations also aim to be well planned, especially those where particular facts, statements, solutions are sought.

In the classroom, systems range from unadulterated impressionistic (e.g. some aspects of art and essays) to clinical analysis of question and answer (e.g. some kinds of maths and science marking). Unfortunately, the criteria for impression marking are not generally stated or indeed statable. An overall 'feeling' of worth is used as the basis for such marks. Many claim that experience teaches them what a piece of work is worth. Research into impression marking is not at all encouraging. Whatever the implicit criteria are, they tend to vary from one marker to the next and very little consistent marking results. At the very least, teachers should attempt to define what it is that gives a good or bad impression, and award marks according to the level of importance of these impressions.

Most teachers use a combination of impression and mark allocation for specified responses in essay-type questions. The problem is that a systematic analysis of questions and answers takes time, but it is time well spent in that it provides a useful framework by which to judge the sources of difficulties – and it assists the teacher in defining what (s)he expects.

In mark-allocation methods (P3, p. 113), there are several issues requiring consideration. What key statements should receive marks? How many marks should be allocated to each point (they may not be of equal importance and therefore should not all receive the same weighting)? Are all the errors the child's fault and therefore should marks be automatically docked? Should some written comment or analysis accompany the mark? What use is going to be made of the response patterns for each child (i.e. if formative or diagnostic, the patterns will be most important; if summative assessment is the case, there need not be any analysis)? How is the mark to be fed back to the pupil (e.g. mark out of ten, grade, written comment only)? What follow up is necessary (e.g. remedial session needed with the class or individuals)? Will the marks form part of course-work assessment? How will progress be judged from one set of marks to the next?

Recording

Most teachers keep a running record of marks awarded to their pupils (P4, below). These are variously used: sometimes they are aggregated to give a continuous assessment/course-work mark; sometimes they form the basis of a written statement of progress; sometimes they are purely for the benefit of the pupil, as in criterion-referencing, to give the pupil an idea of his/her progression; occasionally they are used to provide a projection of subsequent performance (mock 'O' and 'A' levels).

PRACTICE AND OBSERVATION ACTIVITIES

P3   In the final paragraph of the section entitled 'Marking' there are a number of issues which should be investigated on teaching practice or observation. Examine the methods used by teachers in the schools you visit.

P4   Careful and accurate records are essential and students should ensure that they learn as much as they can on teaching practice about record-keeping and its usage.

DISCUSSION AND ANALYSIS ACTIVITIES

D4   The book by Satterly (R1) deals fully with the question of marking and the various problems associated with it. Read the relevant section, and discuss the issues and findings in a tutorial meeting.

REPORTS AND PROFILES

Reports

Common to all schools in our educational system is a reporting method to parents, the local education authority and a school record card which is passed on to the next school attended by the pupil. Writing reports and seeing parents is part and parcel of a teacher's year (D5, p. 117). In this section, we shall look at some findings of a study into school reports at secondary level, although there are general points in this research which are applicable in primary and middle school reporting (R11).

Why do we have school reports? Apart from the accountability exercise which report writing achieves, there are others beyond the classroom who need information about competence which only the class teacher can provide. Progress and potential are necessary pieces of information for parents and employers.

What do reports consist of? The Goacher and Reid study (R11) on school reports came up with about fifteen areas in which teachers most readily comment. To give the student some idea, the list is given below with some examples of typical comments:

	Area of comment	*Typical comment*
1.	Ability	'Above' or 'below average ability'
		'Has a good understanding of this subject'
2.	Attitude	'Enjoys this subject'
		'Has a negative attitude to mathematics'
3.	Behaviour	'Is pleasant and polite'
		'Can be disruptive and rude at times'
4.	Confidence	'Tackles physical education confidently'
		'She tends to be shy and too quiet'
5.	Effort	'Works hard and concentrates'
		Surprise, surprise! 'More effort needed'
6.	Exam results obtained	'A good exam result in physics'
		'Did much more than expected in the written examination'
7.	Homework	'Does his homework diligently'
		'Why does this pupil *never* hand in homework?'
8.	Maturity	'Mary is a mature, responsible prefect'
		'His behaviour is rather silly and he is easily led'
9.	Participation	'Likes to get involved in discussions'
		'Usually stands in the background when there is practical work'
10.	Presentation	'Work is always a pleasure to read – it is so neat'
		'Rather scrappy writer!'

11.	Progress	'John has worked well this term and made exceptional progress'
		'She has not progressed in needlecraft as well as I had hoped'
12.	Prognostic	'Has potential and could do well'
		'I am doubtful as to whether Jean has a future in this subject'

[Adapted from Goacher and Reid (R11). The remaining three areas are remediation, attendance and pastoral comments.]

What types of report do we find in schools (P5 and P6, p. 117)? There are three basic kinds of report. The *single sheet*, which contains all the subjects and space for comments and sometimes marks: the *report book*, which is like single sheets bound together as a booklet; and the *slip report*, where each slip is completed by a teacher and they are compiled afterwards.

Reactions of teachers to reports are most illuminating. These reactions fall into five problem areas.

(a) Subjectivity: it is difficult to be anything but subjective when commenting on some aspects of aesthetic and craft subjects, certain parts of English and the humanities.

(b) Differential performance: problems arise when trying to compare performance in different parts of the same subject. For example, in English is there a valid method of comparing performance in oral work, writing and comprehension; in science, what would be the relationship between practical work, problem-solving and straight descriptive questions?

(c) How does a teacher report honestly without writing demoralising comments? Some particularly poor performers in maths, for instance, are trying hard, but with slow progress (however, compare this with criterion-referencing).

(d) Teachers do sometimes have difficulty in isolating those aspects of a subject to be reported on – in other words, what aspects of performance are incidental and what are central?

(e) Many subject teachers, even in primary schools, where there might be a peripatetic system, might have trouble recalling every pupil taught. This is particularly the case where teachers meet pupils infrequently (religious studies, music).

With regard to (c), many teachers are conscious of the difficulties of giving an objective judgement for low achievers without being discouraging. Learning how to encourage and motivate the pupil with special needs is very important. Teachers, hard pressed for time, never-theless do try to ensure that pupils are set work within their competence, thus ensuring some degree of success.

Parents' reactions to reports are generally favourable. If anything, they want *more* information than is usually provided. They have requested fuller descriptions of *what* the child has learned, the nature of the teaching group the child was in, chances in public examinations, and specific recommendations regarding remedial programmes in which the parent can help.

Profiles

The emphasis of the earlier sections of this chapter has been on academic assessment, but there is a growing realisation that other qualities pos-sessed by children are important and need to be monitored. A research by the Schools Council looked at Profile Reports for School-leavers (R12) (P7, p. 117). The report contains a very full definition of 'profile':

> The term 'profile' ... may be used to describe an internal school assess-ment which includes information on personal qualities, or a pupil-compiled document which may reveal personal qualities and experiences, but the term is more often used to describe a record which gives inform-ation about a wide range of a pupil's attributes. A profile report might include estimated public examination results, levels of competence in basic language and arithmetic skills, assessments of extra-curricular skills such as listening, speaking, manual dexterity, problem-solving, and personal qualities such as initiative and perseverance. [Balogh, R12, p. 7]

As will be revealed shortly, teachers are required to make an extremely wide range of judgements about matters outside the conventional assess-ment of achievement in school subjects. Some examples of profile reports (R12) will quickly show how extensive the teacher's knowledge of pupils would have to be in order to respond to the various sections of the reports. Earlier in the chapter, an example was given of a check list on language skills. Other profiled topics include number skills, study skills, 'life' skills, personal characteristics, health/fitness, interests/achieve-ment, other abilities (scientific, artistic). A useful summary of the main headings is given by Goacher (R12), and these are reproduced in an appendix to this chapter (D6, p. 117). Some of the headings are patently for the school-leaver (e.g. work experience, use of technological language), but most of them can be applied across the school system.

Pupil self-assessment

There is not much research on pupil self-assessment in this country. The Schools Council's work on recording achievement at 16+ (Goacher, R12) is one of the few studies. In this, the pupils were asked to respond to

---

PRACTICE AND OBSERVATION ACTIVITIES

P5 Whenever the opportunity presents itself, try to look at examples of school reports. Discuss the problems surrounding the completion of reports with teachers. Compare their comments with those reported above from the work of Goacher and Reid (R11), which contains examples of school reports.

P6 Many schools provide written guidance on reporting and assessment. You should make enquiries about this in any school you visit. The kind of advice, apart from marking scales, includes completion dates, gradings for effort, achievement, grammatical ability, legibility, neatness and spelling. Keep an eye open for school advice.

P7 Profile reports are becoming an important source of information and will certainly become part of the teacher's routines. You would be wise to discuss this innovation with experienced teachers. What are the advantages? What are the difficulties? (Time-consuming? Subjective judgements about ill-defined psychological and social factors?)

DISCUSSION AND ANALYSIS ACTIVITIES

D5 This whole section on reports is a central one and time should be given in tutorials and method sessions to a discussion of the issues. There should be examples of school reports available and discussion of the problems surrounding their completion.

D6 The book by Balogh (R12) is full of examples of profile reports and this, coupled with Goacher's book, should prove to be a productive starting point for discussions about profiles. Some idea about the content of profiles is given in the appendix to this chapter. Some items on the list are factual (attendance, punctuality); others are very much a question of personal judgement. Discuss in tutorials the limitations of profiles.

---

such questions as 'I can always be relied upon to arrive at school on time' (yes/no) and 'I am normally reliable' (yes/no). Major areas of concern were punctuality, attendance, reliability, perseverance, initiative, participation in lessons, use of numbers and spoken language, understanding speech, reading ability, creativity, dexterity and scientific ability. Teachers were invited to comment on the same range of characteristics for accuracy. The value of these self-assessment devices has still to be shown, but it does help to define for the pupil those attributes which others find of value. Note that the response pattern is typical of criterion-referencing, as the pupils are asked to say with certainty whether they do or do not possess a particular attribute. Some pupils express embarrassment at having to say complimentary things about themselves.

EVALUATING ONE'S TEACHING

In Chapter 1 we claimed that one place to look for ideas about the criteria for judging teaching quality is the training institution's formative and diagnostic inventories for teaching practice. An example was also given of typical criteria.

This book concludes with an example of a diagnostic and a summative assessment schedule in order to inform the student of the kinds of activities about which (s)he must make personal judgements. It is not only a diagnostic tool, but a statement of the requirements of a student on school practice and is thereby a clear indication of what a student should be proficient at when he/she leaves the professional training course. In the student's teaching-practice file, there should be a section for personal evaluation. Some of the criteria in Figure 6.3 should appear in the student's statements about his/her competence (D7).

The assessment in Figure 6.4 is a summative assessment of student performance. It is the basis upon which a final assessment of teaching

---

DISCUSSION AND ANALYSIS ACTIVITIES

D7   Figures 6.3 and 6.4, alongside Table 1.1, should be used as suggested in D2 (p. 9) of Chapter 1 as the basis for a discussion about the syllabus. The points raised in the schedules are patently part of the syllabus and these should be discussed in detail early in the course. Also discuss the relationship between these expectations and the personal comments required from the students.

Lesson topic / context

	Good – Above Average	Satisfactory – Average	Weak – Bare pass	Comments

PLEASE USE SECTIONS SELECTIVELY

Student ....
Respondent ....
Date ....

A Preparation and Planning
1 Clarity of objectives
2 Selection of content appropriate to objectives
3 Student's understanding of content, concepts and skills developed
4 Relevance of content to children's ability and interest
5 Sufficiency of content for the time available
6 Attention to pupil activities in the proposed lesson
7 Creative/interest factor built into planning

B Classroom Performance
1 Exposition of lesson content
2 Clarity of instructions to children / explanations
3 Use of voice; audibility, tone and variation
4 Introduction and use of appropriate materials, e.g. visual aids including blackboard
5 Organisation of materials and resources
6 Appropriate use of questioning at individual and group level
7 Extent to which creative / interest factor accomplished

C Interpersonal Relations
1 Student's ability to achieve rapport with pupils, e.g. warmth, humour
2 Appropriate use of praise and criticism and provision of feedback
3 Attention to the needs of individual children
4 Encouragement and use of pupil contributions during the lesson
5 Anticipation / avoidance of disorderly behaviour
6 Appropriateness of responses to disorderly behaviour
7 Student's ability to obtain pupil attention and participation
8 Overall interaction / involvement of student

D Evaluation
1 Correction of pupils' work and record keeping
2 Quality of pupil's work / pupil's progress
3 Students ability to evaluate effectiveness of own teaching re: planning, preparation and class performance

OTHER COMMENTS

Figure 6.3 Diagnostic assessment of observed lesson. © School of Teacher Education, Humberside College of Higher Education. Reproduced with permission.

Overall assessment of school placement		_____ First / Second	File Copy
		_____ Final	

Student_____   School_____

Respondent _____   Age range taught _____

Date_____   Type of organisation _____

Good – Above Average	Satisfactory – Average – Pass	Fail	
			Grades are composite / summative ones based on diagnostic / formative **lesson schedules** and **general impressions** gained over the whole serial / block period.
			Preparation and Planning including File / Scheme / Lesson plans
			Classroom Performance including displays
			Interpersonal Relations
			Evaluation including recording of pupil's work / progress / adequacy and regularity of marking
			Professional 1 Relations with school staff .... 2 Willingness to teach across a reasonable range .... 3 Interest and involvement across the life of the school .... 4 Willingness to accept responsibility for pupil's learning ....

Further Comment

Figure 6.4   Summative assessment. © School of Teacher Education, Humberside College of Higher Education. Reproduced with permission.

competence is made. It is compiled from several sources, including tutors from the training institutions, teachers in the school on which teaching practice has taken place and who have seen the student teaching or in other roles important to the assessment, and the external examiner in some cases. It is a compressed version of Figure 6.3. I hope these examples of evaluation schedules will serve both students and tutors as a source of information about some of the important aspects of practical teaching which should appear as part of the teacher-training course.

APPENDIX: Profile topics from Goacher (R12)

A. Basic skills

1. *Language*
   (a) Listening
   (b) Speaking
   (c) Reading

   (d) Writing

2. *Numeracy*
   (a) Accuracy
   (b) Calculation
   (c) Measurement

   (d) Graphicacy
   (e) Three-dimensional
       structures

3. *Study skills*
   (a) Remembering
   (b) Presentation
   (c) Ordering/classi-
       fying
   (d) Note-making
   (e) Planning
   (f) Summarising
   (h) Location of
       material
   (i) Working alone
   (j) Group work
   (k) Discussion

B. Personal characteristics

   (a) Attendance
   (b) Confidence

   (c) Co-operation

   (d) Coordination
   (e) Concentration
   (f) Effort/enthusiasm

   (g) Initiative
   (h) Leadership

   (i) Open-mindedness

   (j) Originality/creativity
   (k) Perseverance
   (l) Questioning

   (m) Punctuality
   (n) Relationship
       with peers
   (o) Relationship
       with others
   (p) Reliability
   (q) Self-discipline
   (r) Self-motivation
   (s) Self-reliance

C. Life skills

1. *General*
   (a) Problem solving
   (b) Trainability
   (c) Adaptability
   (d) Coordination
   (e) Practical skills
   (f) Safety consciousness

2. *Specific*
   (a) Use of hand tools
   (b) Use of power tools
   (c) Use of domestic appliances
   (d) Use of telephone
   (e) Form completion
   (f) Sign recognition
   (g) Work experience
   (h) Use of scientific/technological
       language

D. Personal achievements

   (a) Inside school
   (b) Outside school

E. Other possibilities

   (a) Visual skills
   (b) Artistic ability

(*continued on next page*)

(*continued from previous page*)
   (c)   Musical skills
   (d)   Communication skills
   (e)   Understanding society/work
   (f)   Health/physical ability

The preamble to this list in *Recording Achievement at 16+*, by B. Goacher (Longman for the Schools Council, London, 1983, pp. 61–63), is careful to point out that no record *must* include all the items.

REFERENCES

R1   D. Satterly, *Assessment in Schools*, Basil Blackwell, Oxford, 1981.

R2   Norm- and criterion-referencing: *PAT*, Chapter 9, pp. 197–201 and 305–306.

R3   Assessments in use: *PAT*, Chapter 13, pp. 298–310.

R4   Chronological age: *PAT*, Chapter 9, pp. 196–197 and 200.

R5   Mastery learning: *PAT*, Chapter 5, pp. 107–111.

R6   R. Lloyd-Jones and E. Bray, *Assessment: From Principles to Action*, Macmillan, London, 1985. W. Harlen, *Science*, Macmillan, London, 1983. D. Malvern and C. Bentley, *Mathematics*, Macmillan, London, 1983. A. Potton, *Screening*, Macmillan, London, 1983. B. Raban, *Reading*, Macmillan, London, 1983. F.A. Spooncer, *Testing for Teaching*, Hodder and Stoughton, Sevenoaks, Kent, 1984 – particularly for primary schools. E. E. Clough and P. Davis, *Assessing Pupils: A Study of Policy and Practice*, NFER–Nelson, Windsor, 1984.

R7   The National Foundation for Education Research (NFER) produces catalogues from time to time which advertise a range of tests and inventories covering a number of fields. All colleges in teacher education should obtain the catalogue and have a sample kit of the relevant tests available. A particularly useful catalogue is *Educational Guidance and Assessment*, published by NFER–Nelson.

R8   APU Occasional Paper 1, *Learning Mathematics*, Department of Education and Science, London, 1983. Occasional Paper 2, *Foreign Language Provision*, Department of Education and Science, London, 1984. Occasional Paper 3, *Standards of Performance – Expectations and Reality (Science)*, Department of Education and Science, London, 1984.

R9   S. J. Eggleston, *Learning Mathematics*, APU Occasional Paper 1, Department of Education and Science, London, 1983. See *PAT*, Chapter 13.

R10 Cockcroft Committee, *Mathematics Counts*, HMSO, London, 1982.

R11 B. Goacher and M. I. Reid, *School Reports to Parents*, NFER–Nelson, Windsor, 1983.

R12 J. Balogh, *Profile Reports for School-leavers*, Longman for Schools Council, York, 1982. B. Goacher, *Recording Achievement at 16+*, Longman for Schools Council, London, 1983. P. Broadfoot, *Profiles and Records of Achievement*, Holt, Rinehart and Winston, London, 1986. Also see *PAT*, Chapter 13.

Name Index

Subject Index